# Experience Singapore 2016

Len Rutledge

ISBN: 10:153326791X
ISBN-13:978-1533267917

# CONTENTS



All images by Phensri Rutledge unless otherwise indicated

# INTRODUCTION

Experience Travel Guides are unique in that they are designed to be read in the same way as a novel. They are a valuable resource for those planning to visit a destination, a source of information for those just interested in finding out more about a country, and a pleasure for those armchair travelers who just enjoy a good read.

Experience Singapore highlights the visitor attractions so that those planning a visit can quickly and efficiently plan on what they want to see and do. We locate and detail the best places to see and the top experiences to enjoy, and recommend accommodation, shopping and eating options. All are based on the personal experience of the author.

We capture the personality and the underlying cultural and historical significance of the city. Come with us as we explore the wonderful temples, mosques and churches, the few remaining unspoiled natural areas, the historic colonial section, the fantastic shopping opportunities and the exhilaration of the various ethnic zones. Meet a great variety of people, buy the latest gadgets, fashion, and fascinating handicrafts, eat tantalizing cuisine, and enjoy charming hospitality.

As more people travel to new destinations, guide books grow in importance. Hard-copy books, however, are often out of date before they are printed and users are frustrated by experiences contrary to what is described.

This book has no such problem as it can be updated as often as necessary to keep it right up to date. A major update was carried out in March 2016. Be aware that many internet sites provide out of date or inaccurate information. We have done everything possible to ensure our information is up to date and we will continue to update the book as necessary.

Please realize, however, that no guide book can substitute for common sense. Singapore is a hot tropical country so you need to pack clothing, footwear and other items, such as sun protection, appropriate for those conditions.

There are a few restaurants which still require men to wear a jacket but in line with most places in the world, smart casual wear is now considered appropriate for tourists in most situations. Note that many mosques and temples require conservative dress so shorts, rubber shoes and bare shoulders will not be acceptable.

We believe that every place in the world provides unique experiences which make a visit worthwhile. We encourage you to explore, meet the locals and grab each new opportunity as it arises. Travelling is fun but always do it with care and compassion. In that way your Singapore experience can provide lifetime memories.

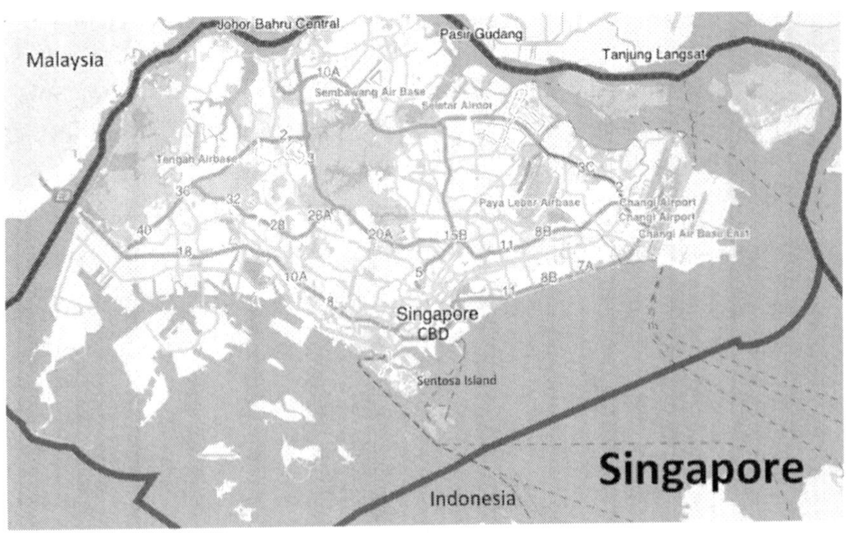

# 1 SINGAPORE – AN INTRODUCTION

Singapore appears as a mere red dot on most maps; a speck at the tip of the Malaysian peninsula. When you realize that the whole country is less than 700 square kilometers or 270 square miles in area, it is really insignificant. The country consists of one main island and about 60 smaller ones and it has two causeway connections to Malaysia. As it sits about 170 km north of the Equator, it is pretty uniformly hot, wet and humid.

Singapore is both a country and a city. A large part of the main island is now residential although it is still possible to find small areas of natural countryside and a few relics of the past. Thirty years ago Singapore embarked on a modernization program that destroyed much of its earlier history and culture but fortunately the mistake was realized just in time and you can still see a few areas which outwardly are little changed in 100 years.

That can be deceiving however, as many of the occupants of old shophouses are IT companies and boutique hotels with an attitude that is as modern as tomorrow.

One of the reasons visitors find Singapore a great place to visit is the blend of cultures that are found there. The largest percentage of the population is Chinese and they believe in hard work, respect for authority and love of family.

The thriving economy, a ruling party that hasn't been beaten since independence, and regular family get-togethers are evidence of this.

The large populations of Malays and Indians have considerable influence on the country's lifestyle while British, other Europeans and Eurasians add further to the mix.

The country currently has a population made up of 76% Chinese, 15% Malay and 6% Indian cultures and the ethnic groups seem to co-exist without much tension. Generally speaking, there is a high level of religious tolerance and racial harmony in this society.

A first-time visitor arriving at modern Changi International Airport, then taking a taxi to the city, would be forgiven for thinking they had arrived at a modern European or international city. The gleaming skyscrapers, wide roads, well-organized traffic and English language provide comfort and confirm that this is a place that is heading for a bright future.

Haji Lane

Universal Studios Singapore

River and Downtown

Chinatown Food Street

Stay a few days and the city's cultural heart will be added to the mix and you will realize that this is a city with a fascinating combination of East and West.

For visitors, the tourist palette is vast. Shopping and eating are local favourite activities and many visitors come to do just that. Singapore was once one of the world's bargain shopping destinations but those days are gone. Now the appeal is in the huge range on offer from the latest world fashion to local and Chinese handicrafts and souvenirs.

Street food was a huge attraction but since all the vendors have been moved into hawker centers, much of the atmosphere has been lost. This make locals concentrate on food flavors and visitors can experience Chinese, Malay, Indian, Peranakan, Indonesian, Thai and Western cuisine in fine restaurants or from small stalls.

While it was once considered a cultural desert, Singapore has responded by creating world-class museums, attractions and casinos. The Asian Civilisations Museum, Singapore Zoo and Night Safari and the Marina Sands complex should not be missed. Hidden gems like CHIJMES, the Lau Pa Sat Pavilion, and the Thian Hock Keng Temple provide unexpected pleasures in what could be a concrete jungle to some people.

While Singapore continues to reach skywards and spreads outwards, places such as the glorious Botanic Gardens, modern Gardens by the Bay, the Bukit Timah Nature Reserve and the Sungei Buloh Wetland provide areas for relaxation and quiet contemplation.

Sentosa Island is something different. It has become a weekend getaway spot for the locals and a fun place for everyone. Recent improvements have seen the establishment of the huge integrated Resorts World Sentosa, Universal Studios Singapore, and people-friendly transport around the island. It is easy to spend a day here and eight hotels provide accommodation for those wanting to stay longer.

It is not just specific attractions that have appeal, however. Different areas of the city offer completely different sights, sounds and smells. The colonial core has history, architecture and stability; the River area has restaurants, nightclubs and its own history; Marina Bay is all new and modern; while Little India, Chinatown and Kampong Glam showcase ethnic cultures in authentic districts. Each area gets its own chapter in the book. A Singapore visit is not complete without a visit to all of them.

Singapore's multi-culture allows various religions to practice their faith in peace. Visitors can visit Chinese and Hindu temples, Western churches and Muslim mosques to see the daily activities held there.

Many of these are in the central areas and even those that are outside this area can be reached by the excellent rail system or the extensive bus network. Both are easy to use once you understand the ticketing arrangements. This is where stored-value fare cards or a Singapore Tourist Pass can be useful.

Visitors will be most comfortable in shorts and T-shirt while touring during the day but for restaurant dining or any business function long trousers and shirt for men and a dress, slacks or skirt and top for women is the appropriate dress. Few places require you to wear a coat or tie except for formal business meetings held in air conditioned offices. Be aware, however, that temples and mosques require you to cover your legs and upper arms when visiting. Some provide robes for this purpose.

Many residents say Singapore is too controlled but visitors are unlikely to experience this feeling. You should be aware, however, that there are fines for littering, spitting, not flushing a public toilet, and making adverse comments about any religion. Selling of chewing gum is illegal so chew mints instead if you need some mouth exercise. The result of all this is some of the cleanest streets in the world. They are also some of the safest.

**Singapore Highlights**

Gardens by the Bay

Night Safari

Singapore Zoo

Botanic Gardens and National Orchid Garden

Sentosa Island

Entertainment at Clarke Quay

Cheap eating at the hawker centers

Shopping in Orchard Road and the Shoppes at Marina Bay Sands

The ethnic enclaves of Chinatown, Little India and Kampong Glam

Jurong Bird Park

Universal Studios Singapore

The buildings and museums of the Colonial Centre

The beaches at Changi, East Coast Park and Sentosa

The churches, mosques and temples

The Marina Bay Sands and Resorts World integrated resorts and casinos

The festivals and events

The luxury hotels

World War II sites and memorials

The nature reserves and wetland areas

# 2 COLONIAL CENTRE AND THE RIVER

This is where colonial Singapore started and it's a great place for visitors to start their exploration of this fascinating city. It is possible to walk to all the places listed in this section although some will find that it becomes a very long day.

I am starting the walk at City Hall MRT station (EW13/NS25). Most of the attractions are to the south and west but there are a couple to the north and east that we can see first.

**Raffles City Shopping Centre** (www.rafflescity.com.sg/) above the station is packed with luxury items in a variety of designer stores such as Omega, Thomas Sabo, and Tommy Hilfiger. There are also Marks & Spencer and Robinson's department stores, fashion chains like Topshop and River Island and excellent restaurants such as Double Bay. It also houses the Swissotel The Stamford Hotel which was the world's tallest hotel when it opened in 1985.

To the east above Esplanade MRT station is **War Memorial Park**. The War Memorial itself stands 61 m tall, and was built to honor those killed during the Japanese Occupation. There are four pillars, symbolizing the Chinese, Eurasians, Indians and Malays. A memorial service is held here each year on February 15 to remember the fall of Singapore to the Japanese in 1942.

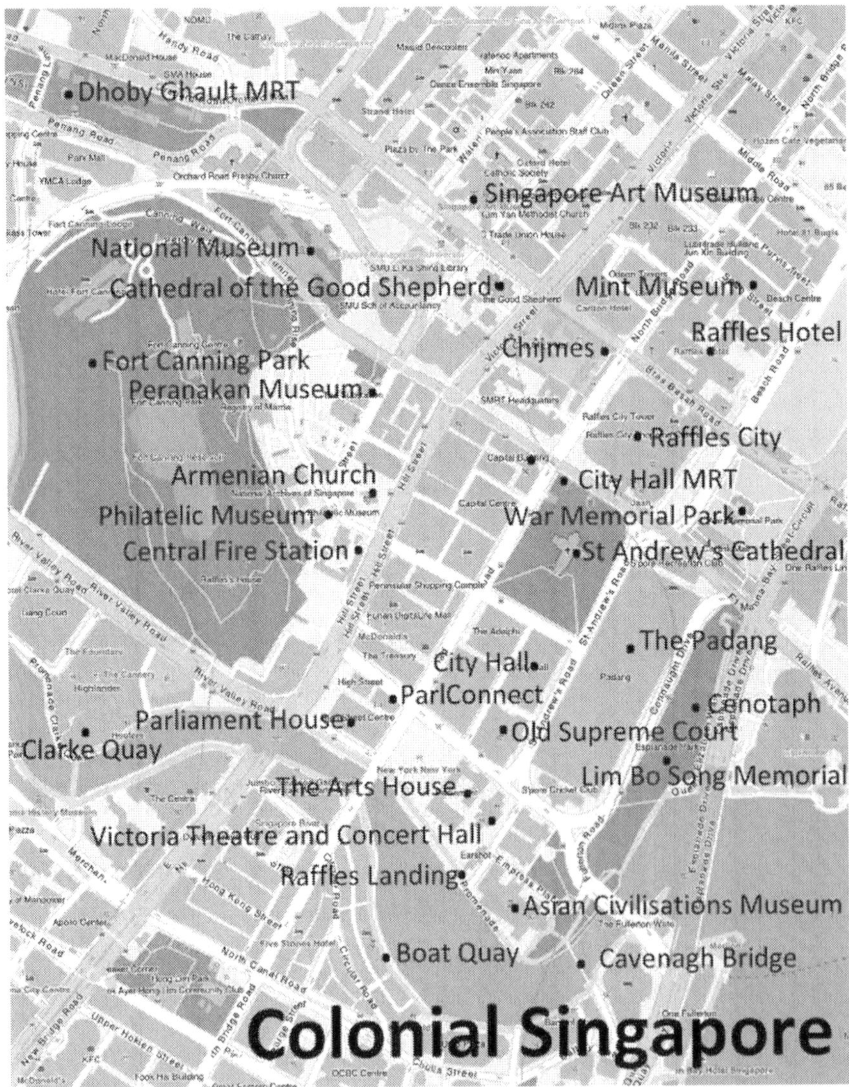


**Raffles Hotel** (1 Beach Road) (www.raffles.com/singapore/) is a Singapore institution not to be missed. Enter from Beach Road into the marbled lobby with its plush Persian carpets, note the wonderful Sikh doorman, and find your way upstairs to the Long Bar for a Singapore Sling. This famous drink was invented here in 1915 and you can still enjoy the great ambiance if you ignore the ridiculous cost.

*Raffles Hotel*

Opened in 1887 by three Armenian brothers who already successfully operated the Eastern and Oriental Hotel in Penang and The Strand in Rangoon, Raffles Hotel has been home to royalty, film stars and writers over the years. It has been beautifully restored to its 1915 appearance and it remains a travel icon.

Even if a Singapore Sling is not on your agenda, walk in the wonderful cool, calm courtyard gardens and make believe you are a celebrity. Don't miss the 1890s ornamental fountain which was made in Scotland and now stands in the Palm Garden.

The **Mint Museum of Toys** (26 Seah St) (www.emint.com/), just beside

Raffles Hotel, opens daily and will appeal to children and some adults. The five-storey contemporary building has been built to house an amazing 50,000-piece toy collection of a local enthusiast. Toys (in the wider sense) come from 40 countries. Many childhood memories will come flooding back to some visitors. Guided tours are available. Entrance is S$15 for adults and S$7.50 for children and seniors.

The museum is also the site for the Mr Punch Public House and its three separate outlets. You can enjoy a meal at the Restaurant, relax with drinks at the Sidewalk Bar, or quench your thirst at the Rooftop Bar with an awesome view of the city.

Go one block north on North Bridge Road to the **Singapore National Library** (100 Victoria St.) which has a very good public and reference library. This 16-storey Library and Theatre complex is well worth a visit for anyone who is interested in the History of Singapore and South East Asia, or if you want to view a great example of public architecture. http://www.nlb.gov.sg/VisitUs/BranchDetails/tabid/140/bid/329/Default.aspx.

The first floor has the main entrance, a large display space and a café. Two outdoor gardens in the library add greenery and a sense of peace. The distinctive red-brick façade of the old building is in one of these gardens. The building has escalators from Basement 3 to the 14th storey and three public panoramic elevators with city views.

The Drama Centre on the third floor adds to Singapore's stable of world-class purpose built performing arts space with its 615-seat proscenium theatre. It also offers an intimate 120-seat black box, and VIP and function rooms to meet the demands of the diverse range of today's arts events.

Across the road from here is the beautifully restored Catholic **St. Joseph Church** (143 Victoria Street) (https://www.facebook.com/St-Josephs-Church-Victoria-Street-Singapore-106219346091155/). It was built in the 1900s in Gothic Style by the Portuguese Mission and it has a beautiful and intricate facade, high wooden ceiling and stained glass windows. The west front has three towers: a central tower with a dome flanked by two smaller towers. The church became a national monument in 2005.

We now head west to the wonderful **Chijmes** complex (30 Victoria Street) (www.chijmes.com.sg/) a jewel of quiet courtyards, cobbled paths and fountains. This was once the Catholic Convent of the Holy Infant Jesus and convent quarters from 1840 known as Caldwell House.

The convent chapel is now a multi-purpose hall known as Chijmes Hall and Caldwell House is an art gallery. Both have been gazetted as national monuments. The complex is now an elegant dining, shopping and entertainment complex that should not be missed. It is particularly attractive at night and you can enjoy live acoustic performances from Sunday to Thursday at the basement 1 courtyard.

Continue west to the **Singapore Art Museum** (71 Bras Basah Road) (www.singaporeartmuseum.sg/) and **SAM at 8Q**.This has an excellent sampling of works by local and south-east Asian artists, and often has visiting temporary exhibitions.

The main museum is housed in an imposing structure built in the early 1880s for the St Joseph's Institution, a school set up by missionaries. You can still see the splendidly restored chapel and the school hall, now called the Glass Hall. The two courtyards are used as exhibition spaces.

SAM at 8Q, around the corner at 8 Queen Street, has expanding the museum's contemporary art space to present painting and sculpture, film & video, photography, new media, performance art and sound art.

Apart from the art there are several cafes on the ground floor at SAM: 7 Kickstart, the Dome Café and Trattoria Lafiandra, and Standing Sushi Bar is located at SAM at 8Q. There are also two shops, the Museum Label on the ground floor at SAM's Waterloo courtyard and Supermama, on the ground floor of SAM at 8Q.

Diagonally across the road is the **Cathedral of the Good Shepherd**, the oldest Roman Catholic Church in Singapore. Built in renaissance style in the 1840s in a Latin-cross pattern, it is the seat of the Catholic Archdiocese. The Cathedral is reminiscent of St Martin's in the Field in London and was gazetted as a national monument in 1973.

There are also three other structures within the compound: the relatively simple Archbishop's House and the more elaborate Resident's Quarters and Priest's House. Cracks appeared in the cathedral's walls, floors and columns in 2006 possibly caused by underground construction works nearby and it is currently closed for major restoration until an estimated mid-2016.

Once you have your fill of the art, wander across the road above the Bras Basah MRT station (CC2) to the **National Museum** (93 Stamford Road) (www.nationalmuseum.sg/) in its Neo-Palladian and Renaissance building**.** The oldest part of the museum is the front block which opened as the Raffles Library and Museum in 1887. An extension block with a 24-metre wide Glass Rotunda, a modern interpretation of the Rotunda Dome in the historic building, was opened in 2006.

This is the nation's oldest museum but it is far from staid and conservative. The galleries adopt cutting-edge ways of presenting history and culture. The museum presents various festivals and events during the year as well as live performances and film screenings.

History is showcased in the Singapore History Gallery while The Singapore Living Galleries celebrate creativity through food, fashion, film and photography. The 10 "Treasures of the National Museum" are not to be missed. Admission to the building is free but foreign visitors pay S$10 for admission to the galleries. The Singapore History Gallery opens from 10 a.m. to 6 p.m. daily while the Singapore Living Galleries open 10 a.m. to 8 p.m. with the last two hours free.

Take a look at the much travelled *Living World* sculpture in the grounds of the museum. This was first placed in front of the National Museum, was moved to the Singapore History Museum's temporary home at Riverside Point, then it moved over to the Singapore Art Museum and finally it has returned to the grounds of the National Museum.

**Fort Canning Park** on Canning Rise is just to the south. The iconic hilltop landmark has witnessed many of Singapore's historical milestones and the hill once sited the palaces of 14th century Malay Kings. Raffles built a house here in 1822 and it was later renamed Fort Canning after the viceroy of India. In 1860 the British built a fort on the hill but this was later demolished to make way for the reservoir. The Gate, the adjoining wall and the Sally Port are all that remain of the fortress.

Archaeological excavations have yielded evidence supporting the existence of the 14$^{th}$ century kingdom of Temasek, later named Singapura ("Lion City" in Sanskrit). The park also holds a tomb said by some to contain the remains of Iskandar Shah, the last ruler of pre-colonial Singapore.

Begin your trail at the Spice Garden, a replica of the first experimental botanic garden in Singapore established by Sir Stamford Raffles. Then go up the hill to the Battle Box, the popular name of the underground command centre constructed as an emergency, bomb-proof command centre during the World War II Malayan campaign and the Battle of Singapore.

The **Battle Box** (http://www.museums.com.sg/about-us/mr-directory/defence/the-battle-box) is now a museum and tourist attraction which is currently closed for renovations until about February 2016.

Don't miss the ASEAN Sculpture Garden where the Philippines, Thailand, Indonesia, Malaysia and Singapore - donated a sculpture to this garden in 1982. Brunei added its contribution in 1988 when it became an ASEAN member.

Fort Canning Park expansive, sprawling lawns play host to concerts, theatre productions and festivals such as Shakespeare in the Park, Ballet

Under the Stars, and Films at the Fort, while weddings, parties and gatherings are a regular sight in the park's venue spaces.

The latest attraction here is the **Singapore Pinacotheque de Paris** (http://www.pinacotheque.com.sg/), which shows works by masters including Amadeo Modigliani, Oscar-Claude Monet and Jackson Pollock. Housed in the historic Fort Canning Art Centre the museum has three gallery spaces: one of which houses a permanent collection rare art pieces, another with a revolving roster of classic and contemporary art, and the last, dedicated to Singapore's history and culture. Tickets start at $7.50

A Singapore Pinacotheque de Paris mobile application is available for both Android and iOS platforms. This works with sensors placed near the artworks to make it possible for visitors to get access to multimedia information within the exhibition.

**Heading back East**

Leaving the Park by way of Canning Rise, we pass close to the **Peranakan Museum** (39 Armenian Street) (www.peranakanmuseum.org.sg/). The building was formerly the Chinese Tao Nan School established in 1906, but this moved in 1982 and the building was restored and opened as the Asian Civilisations Museum.

It was redeveloped in 2008 and re-opened as the Peranakan Museum showcasing elements of the culture that was created by the marriages between Chinese immigrants and locally-born Malays, with a particular emphasis on Singapore, Malacca and Penang.

There are ten permanent galleries showcasing main themes of Peranakan life with many rare and intricate items including teak wedding furniture and distinctive porcelain. The museum opens daily from 10 a.m. to 7 p.m. with an extra two hours on Friday evening.

Admission is S$6 for foreign adults and S$3 for foreign students and seniors.

There is another museum nearby that some will find very interesting. The **Philatelic Museum** (23-B Coleman Street) (https://www.spm.org.sg/) is housed in a 19th century building that was formerly part of the Anglo-Chinese School. The museum's collections include stamps and other philatelic material of Singapore from the 1830s to present day, and stamps from member countries of the Universal Postal Union.

The permanent galleries show how stamps are a window to the world while the museum holds periodic special exhibitions on topics related to current social and cultural trends. Two rooms of particular interest are the Room of Rarities and the Heritage Room. There are both permanent and changing exhibitions and a museum shop. Opening hours are 1 p.m. to 7 p.m. Monday and 9.30 a.m. to 7 p.m. on the other six days. The cost is S$6 for adults and S$4 for children.

Our journey now brings us to Hill Street where there are two attractions. The **Armenian Church** (60 Hill Street) is the oldest surviving Christian church and was the first to be built in Singapore. It was consecrated in1836 and regular Orthodox Christian services continue to be held here. It was gazetted as a national monument in 1973.

The building, which originally featured a domed roof, is a neoclassical design by G D Coleman, the settlement's first qualified architect. The interior of the church is in the traditional Armenian style with its long louvered windows allowing cooling breezes to enter. The grave of Agnes Joaquim, who is remembered in Singapore's national flower, is here.

Across the road is the **Central Fire Station** (62 Hill St), a distinctive red and white Edwardian building from 1901. It houses the Civil Defence Heritage Gallery (http://www.scdf.gov.sg/community-volunteers/visit-scdf-establishments/cd-heritage-gallery) which traces fire fighting and civil defence developments in Singapore from the late 1800s until today.

Admission is free and it opens every day except Monday. Audio-guides are available in English, Mandarin, Malay and Japanese.

The Civil Defence Heritage Gallery Souvenir Shop has a unique collection of gifts consisting of polo T-shirts, printed T-shirts, caps, embroidery badges, pins and other merchandise for fire-fighters.

We are almost back to our starting point as we walk along Coleman Street to **St. Andrew's Cathedral** (11 St Andrew's Road) (http://www.livingstreams.org.sg/sac/index.html). This is undoubtedly the grandest church in Singapore and is probably the most prominent. The original cathedral was demolished in 1852 while the present white Gothic cathedral, which was built by convict laborers, was consecrated in 1862.

The white plaster is said to be a mixture of eggwhite, shell, lime, sugar, coconut husk and water. Note the lancet windows, the turret-like pinnacles, the decorated spires and the large multi-colored stained glass window with a centre panel dedicated to the memory of Sir Stamford Raffles.

The main entrance to the Cathedral is the West Doorway. Above it is the Gallery containing the Walker Pipe Organ. The spire rises 63m and houses the Cathedral's eight bells. The Pulpit which was made in Sri Lanka in 1889 was given to the cathedral by a former Governor, Sir Cecil Smith. The Epiphany Chapel is used for weekday prayers and it incorporates the memorial erected in the original St. Andrew's Church on the same site in 1846.

St Andrew's Cathedral has a wide range of worship services and fellowship group meetings for all ages and languages throughout the week. There are up to 15 services on Sunday in English, Tagalog, Mandarin, Cantonese, Hokkien and Indonesian and there are also services on every other day of the week.

Across Coleman Street is **City Hall (St Andrew's Road) which was c**ompleted in 1929 and was once Singapore's most important government building. It features Grecian architecture, dignified Corinthian columns across its front, two internal courtyards and a grand staircase. This is where the World War II surrender of the Japanese in 1945 occurred and also where the declaration of Singapore's city status in 1951 and the proclamation of self-government by Lee Kuan Yew in 1959 happened.

Next door is the imposing **Old Supreme Court**, the last colonial classical building to be built in Singapore in 1939. It has colossal Corinthian columns and a miniature replica of the dome of St Paul's Cathedral. An allegory of Justice stands above the entrance, as well as a frieze depicting the historic signing of the 1819 treaty between Raffles and Sultan Hussein which established Singapore as a trading post. Note that the granite of the building is actually a type of molded plaster.

Both the old Supreme Court and the City Hall have been extensively remodeled and are now home to the **National Gallery of Singapore**. This opened in November 2015, and displays more than 8000 of the region's most extraordinary art pieces from the 19th and 20th centuries. The gallery offers visitors the world's first and largest insight into South-East Asia's culture and history.

Opening hours are Sunday to Thursday and public holidays 10 a.m.–7 p.m., and Friday and Saturday 10 a.m.–10 p.m. There is free entry for Singaporeans and the standard ticket for non-Singaporeans is $20 with concessions available.

The large green area across St Andrews Road is called **The Padang.** Cricket has been played here as far back as 1837 and the Singapore Cricket Club was established in 1852. The present building is from 1884 and is the third on this site. Cricket, rugby sevens, soccer sevens and hockey sixes have all been played here. The National Day Parade and other events have been held here.

The Singapore Cricket Club (http://scc.org.sg/) today has over 3,000 members and has facilities for squash, tennis, lawn bowls, billiards and snooker. Reciprocal rights exist with many significant clubs around the word. The web-site gives details. Numerous dining options are available here.

To the east of the Padang is the **Cenotaph**. This was unveiled in 1922 in memory of those Singaporeans who died in World War I. A dedication to those who died in World War II has been added to the reverse side of the monument. In the same area just to the south, is the **Lim Bo Song Memorial** dedicated to Major-General Lim Bo Seng, an outstanding

World War II hero who led the anti-Japanese resistance movement and was killed by the Japanese.

## Along the River

Our wanderings have brought us to the Singapore River near pedestrianised **Cavenagh Bridge**, Singapore's oldest and only suspension bridge. You can look across to the south bank, now laden with skyscrapers, mainly associated with the banking industries.

We will stay on the north bank of the river because there are a variety of attractions along here. The first is the **Dalhousie Obelisk** built in 1850 to honor the visit of Lord James Andrew, the Marquise of Dalhousie, then-governor-general of India. The Obelisk was Singapore's first public monument.

Nearby is the **Asian Civilisations Museum** (1 Empress Place) (https://www.acm.org.sg/) in a neoclassical building built in 1867 as a Court House. For many years it housed various Government departments then became the Empress Place Museum in 1989 and after a major renovation it opened in its present form in 2003. This is an extremely well-presented museum and is probably the museum I most enjoy in Singapore.

There are some fine artifacts and exhibits here showing how Singapore's multi-cultural society has developed from various pan-Asian cultures and civilizations. Through a collection of works of art and a varied exhibition program, the museum will deepen your understanding of south-east Asia, China, south Asia and the Peranakan world. The museum shop has some excellent ethnic crafts which make excellent gifts. The museum opens daily from 10 a.m. to 7 p.m. with late Friday closing at 9 p.m.

As part of Singapore's 50th-anniversary celebrations two new wings that bring light and space to the museum have been opened with a look that contrasts yet complements the original neoclassical façade. This has further increased the appeal of the whole museum.

Immediately to the west is one of Singapore's most historic sites. **Raffles Landing Site** is where Thomas Stamford Raffles, an agent of the British East India Company, is believed to have landed in 1819. He was hoping to establish a free port midway along the China-India trade route. Raffles signed a treaty with the Johore Sultan and Singapore's rise to statehood began. Today a white polymarble statue of Sir Stamford Raffles stands at this spot.

Behind the Landing Site is the **Victoria Theatre and Concert Hall,**

(https://www.nac.gov.sg/arts-spaces/nac-arts-venues) a complex of two buildings and a clock tower which have been joined together. The splendid 1862 Victorian-era colonial theatre and the 1905 hall with its distinctive Palladian clock tower, Italianate windows and rusticated columns has been a town hall, hospital and a war crimes trials court.

During WWII, the clock was set to Tokyo time when Japan occupied the island. The ballots for Singapore's first election were counted here in 1954, and the government led by Lee Kuan Yew's People's Action Party was inaugurated here.

Today this is a lively venue for the performing arts. The grand old dames of Singapore's performing arts scene reopened in 2014 after a three-year refurbishment costing $158 million. The existing theatre and concert hall has been transformed into intimate spaces, designed to provide an engaging experience between audiences and the performers. Check www.sistec.com.sg for event information and ticketing. The original bronze statue of Stamford Raffles now stands to the front of the building.

Moving west we now come to **The Arts House** (1 Old Parliament Lane) (https://www.theartshouse.sg/). This was built in 1827 as a private residence by G. D. Coleman, an architect who contributed greatly to early Singapore, and it is the city's oldest surviving building. It was used as a court, Government offices, and Singapore's first parliamentary building.

It was originally built in the neo-Palladian style but was later transformed into an eclectic French classical style. Today, it houses the Arts House, a multi-disciplinary arts centre. The former Parliamentary Chamber is the highlight of The Arts House, and is now a popular venue for musical performances, stage productions and conferences. Other venue options include a black box theatre, galleries, multi-purpose rooms, and a screening room.

Outside the building is a bronze statue of an elephant which was a gift from King Chulalongkorn of Thailand when he made his first overseas visit to Singapore in 1871.

The next building is the present parliament building. This has an interesting free Visitor Centre, named **ParlConnect** (Parliament Place) (https://www.parliament.gov.sg/parlconnect-bringing-parliament-closer-people) for walk-in visitors who wish to find out more about the Singapore Parliament. It provides a public access point for visitors to learn about the various aspects of the Parliament, through its interactive features and multimedia displays and opens every weekday.

You can surf the Parliament website, listen to landmark debates, watch an educational video, and view photographs and documents. There is also a shop, which sells a variety of parliamentary souvenirs and publications related to the work and development of Parliament. When Parliament is sitting, you can also access the visitors' gallery from here.

The new **Parliament House** (1 Parliament Place) (https://www.parliament.gov.sg/visiting-parliament-house), with its distinctive "colonnade" design features, was opened in 1999. Consisting of three new blocks and a restored colonial building, its dignified and stately appearance is appropriate for its purpose.

The other side of the river from all these majestic buildings is **Boat Quay**. The row of shophouses here used to be a hub of commerce and trade but now they provide a great destination for al fresco dining and drinking, with restaurants and pubs lining the promenade. But it's not just for eating and drinking. From massages to yoga to fine dining or catching a cooking class, this tiny enclave has something for everyone.

Reclaimed from swamps in 1822, Boat Quay was the first area along the Singapore River developed to provide commercial and warehousing facilities for the thriving centre. The original structures were mostly two-storey buildings with simple facades but over time, they evolved into buildings incorporating Eastern and Western features and styles. It is now a designated conservation area and is great for a slow wander.

Not to be missed is the series of life-like bronze sculptures called "People of the River". They depict some of the characters who developed Singapore in the early days.

**1-Altitude Viewing Gallery** (1 Raffles Place) (www.1-altitude.com/) is a viewing gallery on the roof of the OUB Centre. It offers a 360-degree view of Singapore from the highest point in the city-state at 282m. You are provided with hi-tech gadgets which allow you to see information about the places you are looking at. In the same building you will find **Fitness First Platinum** (http://www.fitnessfirst.com.sg/), consisting of a compact little gym, a rooftop swimming pool, two Jacuzzis and a tennis court. Day passes are available but it is closed on Sundays.

Further west we come to **Clarke Quay**. Space constraint at Boat Quay by the 1860s meant that new *godowns* and factories had to be built further upriver so Clarke Quay was developed. The quay is named after Sir Andrew Clarke, the Governor of the Straits Settlements from 1873 to 1875.

In recent years it has become one of Singapore's best dining and entertainment destination; a colourful kaleidoscope of buildings housing antiques, restaurants, hip cafes, jazz clubs and more. At night, five blocks of restored warehouses light up with an array of quirky places to visit.

A promotion called Alive After 5 has outlets offering complimentary drinks, special promotions and one for one offers during happy hour. If you are not into drinking you can enjoy being photographed amongst the water jets that shoot up from the floor of the Clarke Quay central hub.

There are also moored Chinese junks that have been refurbished into floating pubs and restaurants, and the G-Max reverse bungee which offers thrill-seekers a unique experience. The quay is a major starting point for river cruises and water taxis. You can cruise down to Marina Bay and take a voyage through time by following the journey of Singapore from the days of Raffles though the dreams of her people to the amazing results of their imagination.

You are now within easy walking distance of the Clarke Quay MRT station (NE5) but if you are still up for more walking you can continue west along River Valley Road to the **Chettiar Temple** at the corner of Tank Road. This is a modern Hindu temple which is one of the wealthiest and grandest in Singapore. There is a five-storey entrance archway, massive patterned rosewood doors and prayer halls decorated with sculptures. A further highlight is the ceiling which has etched glass panels of gods.

If you want to return to an MRT station, walk north along Tank Road towards Orchard Road. Here you will pass The **Church of the Sacred Heart** (111 Tank Road), a Roman Catholic property founded in 1910 by the Society of Saint Vincent de Paul. In 2008, the church was renovated and a 7 storey community building housing meeting, catechism and prayer rooms, priest offices, music studio, car parks, and a new cafeteria was built. Dhoby Ghault MRT station (CC1/NE6/NS24) is close by.

# 3 CHINATOWN AND OUTRAM PARK

Chinatown remains a popular area for visitors although much of the area has been demolished and redeveloped and hence it has lost some of its genuine appeal. Fortunately some areas have been spared and these today offer a nice mixture of historical structures and restaurants and shops. It is safe and accessible, and is a great place for walking.

Strange Chinese medicines, questionable antiques, and cheap souvenirs may tempt you to buy but this is also just an area for wandering. There are many shrines, museums and other cultural buildings, for history or religious buffs.

From its earliest beginnings as an ethnic enclave for Chinese immigrants, Chinatown has always been an important part of the Singapore landscape. Chinatown was an entertainment centre in the early 19$^{th}$ century when it was alive with storytellers, buskers, brothels, opium dens and roadside hawkers. Much of this has now gone but the bustling ambience can still be felt. It is a place where tradition meets modernity and Chinese medicinal shops sit comfortably besides spas and bars.

Chinatown is a great place to visit anytime but it takes on a special ambience during Chinese New Year (Late January or early February). Most people will dress in red and give children *AngPow*, a monetary gift in a red packet to bring luck and prosperity. Every household is busy with spring cleaning to get rid of the old and welcome the new.

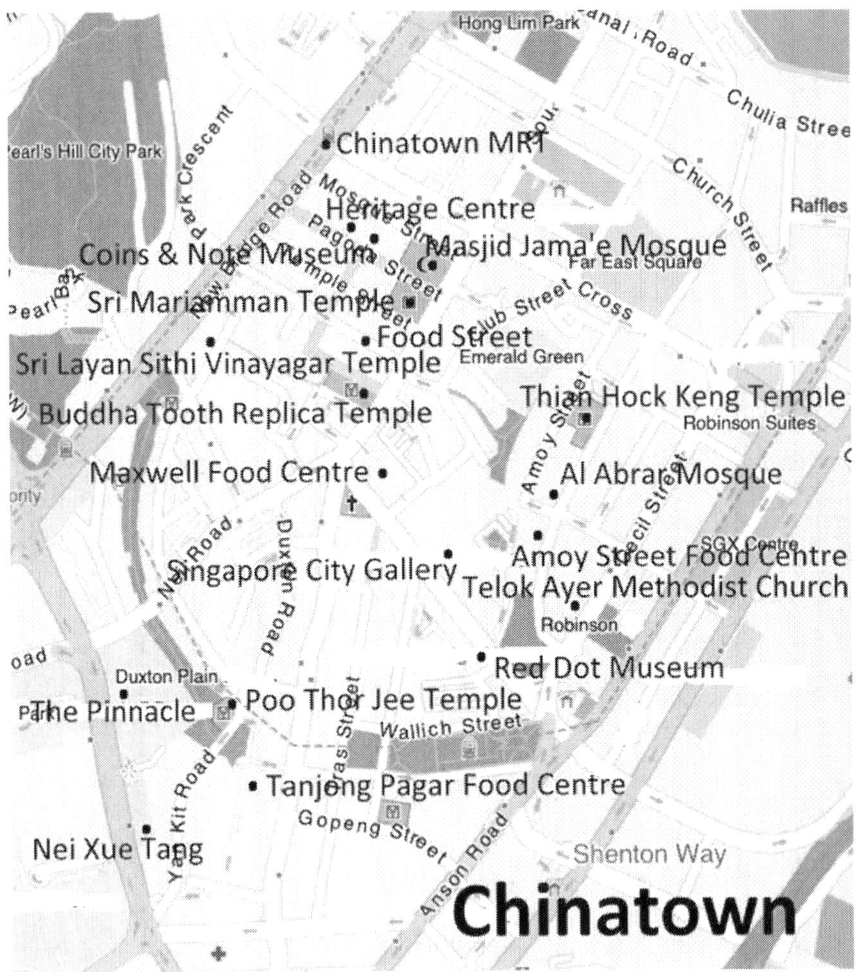


Houses are decorated in red and people celebrate with fire crackers. It is believed that these chase off evil spirits and awakens the deities and guardian spirits who are the custodians of good health, good fortune and prosperity.

Walking tours are available for those who feel they need help but you can easily wander around by yourself and see the sights and sounds that make this place unique. It is probably a good idea to visit the **Chinatown Visitor Centre** located at Kreta Ayer Square just behind the Buddha

Tooth Relic Temple. This new Visitor Centre built by the Chinatown Business Association serves up information about Chinatown's shops, history, culture and more.

Footprint of our Forefathers is a free walking tour which lets you explore Chinatown and hear about the stories of Chinatown. A free food sampling is provided to let you have a taste of the local delicacies at the Chinatown Food Street. It's advisable to wear a comfortable pair of shoes and outfit. This is a rain or shine event every Saturday at 9.30 a.m. to 11.30 a.m. which leaves from the Chinatown Visitor Centre.

I am starting my wanderings at the Chinatown MRT station (NE4/DT19). Most of the attractions are to the south and east but before going in those directions it is worth checking out the large shopping centers along New Bridge Road right outside the station. People's Park Centre, Yue Hwa and the adjacent OG People's Park, and Chinatown Point occupy three corners of the New Bridge Road and Upper Cross Street intersection.

Inside these complexes are shops selling electronics, clothing, textiles,

Chinese medicine, religious icons, handicrafts, cosmetics and jewelry. You will also find local food such as barbecued meat, traditional Chinese sausage and much more. These complexes are not the same standard as most along Orchard Road but prices are excellent, although quality varies.

Across the road from the People's Park Complex is Pagoda Street where in earlier days opium dens and slave traders thrived. Today these have been replaced by shops, restaurants and the **Chinatown Heritage Centre** (48 Pagoda St.) (http://www.chinatownheritagecentre.sg/). This is an extremely interesting place inside three old shophouses, with old photographs, videos and exhibits covering the dangerous journey across the South China Sea and life in the then-British colony.

The Centre reopened in January 2016 after extensive renovations. Much of the museum is given over to recreating the cubicle living of early Chinatown. Each 8 x 4 meter cubicle recreates the living space of different families, shops and trades. You can enter a number of the cubicles and be guided by the very good guide book issued with your ticket. The top floor tells the tale of Chinese migration to Singapore in the 19th and 20th century and the development of modern Singapore.

The centre opens every day with a current admission charge of Adult S$15, Child S$11. A guided tour at extra cost is offered. The attached Chinatown Heritage Restaurant serves good Chinese food and the gifts from the shop are generally of higher quality than you'll find in the street market.

We continue to walk along Pagoda Street and come to the **Masjid Jama'e Mosque** (218 South Bridge Road), an Indian Muslim mosque built in 1826 by Chulia Muslims from India's Coromandel Coast. It was designed by early Singapore architect George Coleman and is a marriage of East and West.

The front gate is typical of southern Indian mosques, there are Malay influences in the timberwork and much of the building is in the neoclassical Western style. You are welcome to enter provided you observe the modest dress code and remove your shoes.

Across on the other corner is the **Sri Mariamman Hindu Temple** (244 South Bridge Rd.) built in 1823 by a government clerk who had followed Raffles from Penang. This is a national monument and a major tourist attraction in Chinatown.

The temple, which is topped by a pagoda-shaped tower at its main entrance, is dedicated to Goddess Mariamman. There is no admission charge but you have to pay a fee if you want to take a picture or video while inside the temple. After removing your shoes, note the ornate painted ceiling, statuary and altars, where devotees place their offerings. During Theemidhi (in October or November), you can see an amazing fire-walking spectacle.

Temple Street runs along the other side of the temple. It is lined with traditional Chinese medicine stores, karaoke joints and cheap massage parlors in pretty old buildings. Go along here to Trengganu Street then turn left to Smith Street. On this corner is Lai Chun Yuen a former Cantonese opera house. It was built in 1887 and is worth seeing for its lovely latticed balcony railings and graceful columns.

Trengganu Street was once known as Japanese Street because the island's Japanese brothels were concentrated here. Today they have been replaced by hotels, shops and many market stalls. Many shops sell exactly the same goods but watch the quality. There are almost as many food stalls as shops and it's a great opportunity to try some Chinatown favorites.

The market is bustling with activity all day and is particularly attractive when decorated in the months leading up to Chinese New Year.

The modern high-rise Chinatown complex is on another corner of this intersection. Part of this is an indoor market with a wet market in the basement and shops and a hawker centre elsewhere. There is a bewildering variety of fresh produce on display here. Behind this is

Keong Saik Road. Of interest here is the **Sri Layan Sithi Vinayagar Temple** at the corner of Kreta Ayer Road. This is a Hindu temple of the Chettiar community which was built in 1925. You are welcome to visit.

Across the road is the Hotel 1929, named after the year the building was built. The original façade of the shophouses hides an ultra-modern interior. Shophouses were mostly built with two or three stories, with a shop on the ground floor and a residence above. Many have a covered walkway which is within the shophouse property line but is for public use, providing pedestrians with shade from sun and protection from rain.

This whole area was once famed for its red lanterns and ladies of the night. As you walk the streets around here you will see several buildings restored to their original architectural splendor with timbered ceilings, shutters and louvered doors. It is one of the few areas remaining where you can see the color, character and charm of a bygone era.

Eventually we come to Neil Road where, at No.9, **Tea Chapter** (http://teachapter.com/) is a worthwhile experience. You can discover the ancient etiquette associated with tea. The shop surroundings are adorned with calligraphy, paintings and art pieces while gentle music adds to the cozy atmosphere. It is customary to remove your shoes before entering to promote total relaxation and to feel at home.

You are likely to be asked if you need guidance in brewing tea. If so, the serving staff will then run through the whole process from brewing to appreciating tea. I have always been happy with my visits here although the price of around S$20 seems high but I have recently heard complaints about service and attitude. It opens daily until mid-evening.

Walking north you soon reach Sago Lane which was once lined with death houses. The old Chinese believed that dying in the house you lived in brought bad luck to those who remained, and so many came here to die. As part of funeral rituals, paper effigies of worldly goods were burned to make sure similar comfort would go with the deceased to the spirit world.

Although death houses no longer exist in Singapore, you'll still find shops selling elaborate and intricate paper effigies of valuable objects such as cars and credit cards; but not here. Instead there are shops and restaurants engaged in the food or retail businesses.

We now reach another major Chinatown attraction, **The Buddha Tooth Relic Temple and Museum** (288 South Bridge Rd) (www.btrts.org.sg/), a massive Tang Dynasty-influenced structure completed only in 2007. It is said that a relic from the Buddha's tooth is housed inside. Hundreds of miniature golden Buddha statues line the walls of the temple. You are free to walk around the temple and there is no charge.

Start in the 100 Dragons Hall on the first floor before spending time in the Buddhist Culture Museum located at the 3rd level. Don't miss the golden stupa on the fourth floor which supposedly encases the sacred tooth, and the Tibetan prayer wheel and orchid garden on the roof.

Go one street north and we are back to Smith Street. This is the **Chinatown Food Street** (http://chinatownfoodstreet.sg/) which has just undergone a complete refurbishment. Newly constructed high-ceiling glass canopy shelters allow diners to enjoy the outdoor dining regardless of rain or shine. There are lots of choices between essentially hawker stands and sit down restaurants.

This is a great place for first time visitors to experience a variety of local dishes at reasonable prices but be aware that it is a mishmash of authentic Chinese food outlets and tourist traps. This is one of the few places in town where you can actually eat street food on the street or in adjacent shophouse restaurants. There is great choice including grilled satay, barbequed seafood, and the ever popular char kway teow — a stir-fry of prawns, cockles, sausage, rice noodles, and lard.

It is worthwhile to cross South Bridge Road to sample some famous egg tarts from Tong Heng (285 South Bridge Road). Just north is Singapore's oldest traditional Chinese medicine hall occupying three wonderfully restored Art Deco-style shop-houses.

We now need to get to Club Street which more or less parallels South Bridge Road to the east. This was once the home of Chinese social clubs, shophouses, and brothels but it has been turned into a trendy neighborhood with boutiques, bars, and clubs with colorful shopfronts, old window shutters and streetlamps from a by-gone era.

There is beautiful architecture and elegantly-restored classic details like traditional gate grills, intricate latticework and charming balconies. On a few building you will see green ceramic roof tiles resembling bamboo stems, which are supposed to direct the flow of rainfall, a symbol of prosperity, over the front of the house.

Singapore's main commercial district from 1850 to 1870 was along Telok Ayer Street, a few streets to the east, which once bordered the original shoreline. Ann Siang Hill Park is an idyllic spot with a timber trellis, some swings and seating pavilions, and a well at the bottom of the staircase.

There are many temples and mosques in this vicinity. One that remains in daily use is the **Thian Hock Keng Temple** (158 Telok Ayer St). It is one of the oldest temples in Singapore, the most important for the Hokkien Chinese Buddhists, and a place that I believe should not be missed.

A simple building was constructed here in 1821 while the present masterpiece with stone columns, wooden carvings and tile mosaics was constructed a few decades later. The gates were imported from Scotland, the facade tile came from the Netherlands, and all the other building materials came from China.

The statue of Ma Zu Po, goddess of seafarers, was imported from China in 1840 and is in the main hall. The ceiling here is spectacular with gilded carvings depicting stories from Chinese folklore, animals, flowers and war heroes. There are twin dragons on the temple's roof ridge and a glass globe that represents the sun.

On the same street is the **Al-Abrar Mosque** (192 Telok Ayer St.) which was originally built in 1827 by Indian moneylenders as a simple thatched building. Today's building with its two minaret-style towers, comes from the 1850s although it underwent major renovations in the late 1980s. It was designated a national monument in 1974.

We now walk south to McCallim Road then go west to The Club Hotel (28 Ann Siang Rd) a 22-room luxury boutique hotel. Housed in a stately 1900's heritage building, the design has a stylish blend of contemporary minimalism and antique, oriental highlights. Just around the corner is The Scarlet (33 Erskine Road) another popular hotel with plush features and opulent décor.

Other properties still retain their original flavor and you can peep discreetly through open windows or doors to glimpse ancestral portraits and hear the click-clack of a mahjong game in progress.

The **Maxwell Food Centre** (1 Kadayanallur St) is a popular place for trying a cross-section of the local food. When I last visited I was surprised and disappointed by the amount of rubbish and uncollected bowls and plates but it is less of a tourist trap than other places like Newton Food Centre.

Apparently Singaporeans don't return trays or used bowls to a central point so due to staff shortages they build up on the tables. It is not a good look. One big asset of this place is that it trades late so you can pick up a 2 a.m. snack after a night out. The best Chicken Rice in the market (and I think in Singapore) is at Tian Tian Hainaneese Chicken Rice.

Across the road at the corner of Neil and Tanjong Pagar is a two-storey brick building that was once the city's centre for rickshaws (*jinrikshas*). The building has a square tower with an octagonal cupola, and a delightfully sunny central courtyard.

Along Maxwell Road is the **Singapore City Gallery** (URA Building, 45 Maxwell Rd) (https://www.ura.gov.sg/uol/citygallery) which has flashy video presentations on the ground floor and city planning simulators, models of Singapore's physical growth from land reclamation, and a miniaturized city model on the next level. I find this place very interesting and admission is free but others may say it has little interest to them. It opens Monday to Saturday from 9 a.m. to 5 p.m.

One thing not to miss here is the Light and Sound Show which occurs on a huge model of the central city area. The show is supposed to be on the hour in English but was out of action when I last visited.

Behind here is the **Amoy Street Food Centre** (7 Maxwell Road) which offers a lot of food variety from around the world. The prices there are very reasonable, and it's usually packed during lunch time.

The **Telok Ayer Chinese Methodist Church** (http://www.tacmc.org.sg/) is just across Telok Ayer Road. It was built in 1924 and is unusual because of its traditional Chinese roof and large Byzantine windows. The basic design is western; a rectangular main body sitting on arch colonnades, but there is an open pavilion on the roof at the front of the building with a roof carved in the traditional Chinese manner.

Now let's cross Maxwell Road and visit the **Red Dot Museum** (28 Maxwell Rd.) (www.museum.red-dot.sg/) a quirky place in an old red police barracks. Singaporeans often call their island 'the little red dot' hence the name of the museum. You can see the latest trends in the international design scene with a collection of more than 1,000 exhibits in the field of product design and communication design from over 50 countries.

Items on display vary from mundane objects to those that show truly outside-the-box thinking. If you are a design buff you will love this place. Admission is S$8 adults and S$4 for seniors, students and children. The Design Museum Shop has a wide collection of design objects and gifts that are frequently found only at the shop and not elsewhere in Singapore.

Entrance is free to the museum on the first Friday of the month when the museum hosts an artists' market called MAAD [Market of Artists And Designers] which is claimed to be the largest monthly creative market in Asia.

We have left Chinatown now and are in the Tanjong Pagar area where the attractions are more spread out. There is no obvious tour route from here but it is worth finding the **Poo Thor Jee Temple** (7 Yan Kit Rd), a Buddhist temple that houses the Zhuan Dao Buddhist Library & Cultural Arts Centre. The temple was founded in 1911 at Narcis Street but was rebuilt in 1968 at the current site. The cultural centre was opened in 1995.

Nearby is the **Tanjong Pagar Food Centre** and the Tanjong Pagar Plaza. The food centre is notable for its local dishes such as nasi leak and fish soup. In all food centers I go to the stalls which have the longest lines as the locals know which are the best outlets.

At the end of Nan Kit Road is **Nei Xue Tang** (235 Cantonment Rd) (www.neixuetang.org/visitorinformation.aspx) a privately owned Buddhist art museum. The museum was created by collector Woon Wee Teng and is located in a four-storey pre-war house built in the Peranakan style. There are many special and interesting features about the building so the premises have been conserved for heritage and architectural reasons.

The collection showcases significant Buddhist artifacts, relics, antiquities and works of art coming from Japan, China, Thailand, Cambodia, Indonesia and elsewhere. The items collected for display are of different medium and there are gold, silver, bronze, stone, horns, jade, crystal and others. The museum opens from 10 a.m. to 5 p.m. daily with admission of S$5 for adults and S$3 for children over 8 years of age. Younger children are not permitted.

*Board games are still popular with the older men*

Further west on Cantonment Road is **The Pinnacle@Duxton Skybridge** (1G Cantonment Rd) (www.pinnacleduxton.com.sg/Public.html). There is a viewing deck on the 50th floor of Singapore's tallest public housing project that offers some of the best city views for a cost of S$5. Go to

Tower G, level one and there you will find the office where the security guard monitoring the screens will issue you a ticket.

Seven buildings in this complex are all connected by promenades at the 26th and 50th floor levels. Visitors are permitted on the 50th floor section and you are free to stay as long as you like. It has a great view of Sentosa and the Chinatown and Duxton Hill areas, however, you don't see any of the iconic central Singapore skyline. I would highly recommend coming on a weekday since weekends tend to be somewhat crowded.

**Everton Park** is a cluster of six old public apartment blocks opposite The Pinnacle. There is an array of old-style shops and restaurants with an increasing number of hipster joints opening right alongside them. It is a great place to see how old and new Singapore co-exists.

Look up and you'll see washing on bamboo poles out the windows; you'll see small doors too, which used to be central rubbish chutes.

Walk further west to Everton and Blair Roads which house some of the finest groups of Peranakan-style shophouses in the city. Many are nearly a century old and have been refurbished for modern use. Unlike many of the other shophouses in other parts, the ones here are still used for residential purposes.

**Baba House** (157 Neil Rd) (www.nus.edu.sg/cfa/museum/about.php) is a showcase of the distinctive Peranakan culture now belonging to the National University of Singapore. It has an elaborate, original interior. This was once the ancestral home of a wealthy Straits Chinese family and you can see how they lived through the restoration of interiors including furnishing, household materials and decorative features.

Entry is free though appointments need to be made in advance via the web site. One-hour Heritage tours are available on Monday, Tuesday, Thursday and Saturday at specific times and these also need to be booked.

A final stop should be made at the bold New Majestic Hotel (31-37 Bukit Pasoh Road) as we walk to the Outram Park MRT station (EW16/NE3). It is idiosyncratic in the extreme and features rooms designed by the city's biggest creative names. See the collection of vintage Compton fans and furniture in the gleaming terrazzo lobby and the eccentric artworks in every nook and cranny. This is the new Singapore set within a 1920s building. I just hope the pool doesn't leak!

There are many tours available within Chinatown. I have little personal knowledge of any of them but the Chinatown Food Tour is worth considering. You visit a hawker complex and a hawker centre and learn the difference between them. You try an array of amazing food including the popular chicken rice, and you also visit the Singapore City Gallery. It is a way to learn a little more about Singapore in an enjoyable way.

# 4 MARINA BAY AREA

Marina Bay is something of a misnomer these days as the body of water is no longer open to the sea. It has been formed by large areas of reclaimed land and is controlled by the Marina Barrage which acts as a barrier to prevent flooding on high tides. The bay is thus a fresh water storage which is used to supplement the city's water supply.

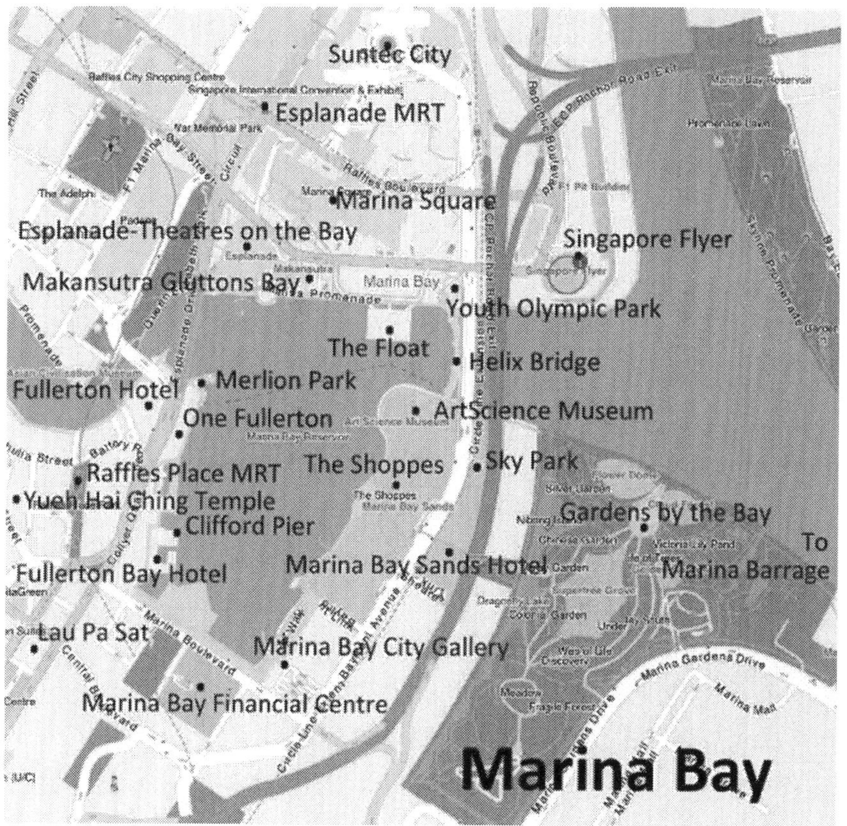

Our walk today starts at the Raffles Place MRT station (EW14/NS26). This could be called Singapore's Central business District with its high-rise towers and financial focus. Note the entrance to the station which has detailing reminiscent of the John Little Department Store Building's facade dated 1911 which was fashioned in a Spanish style.

**Raffles Place** is an open-air plaza surrounded by skyscrapers including the twin-tower UOB Plaza, the twin-tower One Raffles Place which was once the tallest building in the world outside North America, Republic Plaza, One Raffles Quay and OCBC Centre. There are two sculptures on the ground floor of the UOB Plaza that are worth seeing; *Homage To Newton* by Salvador Dali and *Bird* designed by Columbian Fernando Botero.

The original Commercial Square on this site was renamed Raffles Place in 1858. Banks and other commercial establishments had grown up around the square but much was destroyed during World War II by Japanese bombing. A further disaster occurred in 1972 when the Robinson's Department Store fire completely destroyed one of Singapore's legendary landmarks killing at least nine people.

In the midst of all this modern development is the **Yueh Hai Ching Temple** (30B Phillip St), Singapore's oldest Taoist temple. It is believed it was first constructed around 1826, and was rebuilt in 1895.

The temple has been recently renovated and you should see the ceramic figurines and pagodas adorning the roof, and the tiny three-dimensional reliefs that depict scenes from Chinese operas in every nook and cranny of the structure. Also see the large incense coils hanging in the courtyard.

A complete contrast to these modern and ancient structures is provided by the slightly downstream **Fullerton Building**, named after the first Governor of the Straits Settlements. Built in 1919 as an office building, the General Post Office occupied the two lower floors while the exclusive Singapore Club rented premises on the upper floors. From

1958 to 1978, a lighthouse beacon on the building's rooftop guided vessels approaching the harbor.

When the Post Office, vacated the building in 1996 it was convert into the 400-room luxury Fullerton Hotel Singapore which commands a spectacular vista of the Civic District as well as Marina Bay.

Go under Fullerton Road and you reach **Merlion Park** (www.yoursingapore.com/see-do-singapore/recreation.../merlion-park.html). This park beside the Esplanade Bridge has been home to the popular statues of the Merlion and a Merlion cub since 2002. They were originally located at the mouth of the Singapore River when built in 1972, and have since become a Singapore tourism symbol.

Visitors still flock here so you may have to wait in line to get a good photograph. The view across Marina Bay from here is quite impressive with several interesting waterfront architectural structures being highlights.

Jubilee Bridge provides a friendly, barrier-free connection between the Merlion Park and the waterfront promenade in front of the Esplanade. The 220-metre bridge offers a panoramic vista of the historic Civic District to the east and of the Central Business District and Marina Bay to the west.

Behind the park is the low-rise **One Fullerton** complex which contains some of Singapore's best restaurants, bars and entertainment outlets. There are chic cafes and fine-dining alfresco restaurants serving a variety of International cuisines.

It's a long but very interesting walk around the bay from here. As we go south we first encounter what remains of **Clifford Pier**. Built in 1933, this was a landing point for sea passengers. The pier was later used as a terminal for ferries heading for Singapore's small southern islands. Clifford Pier was closed 2006, and was replaced by the Marina South Pier which is on the sea outside the barrage.

*Merlion and City Skyline*

When Clifford Pier first opened, hawkers on sampans offered porridge and simple dishes to those arriving by ship. Now the pier has been incorporated into the Fullerton Bay Hotel and a stunning new restaurant here pays homage to Singapore's hawker food culture with dishes such as Soup Kambing, Porchetta, and Massaman Lamb Rack. It is no longer cheap but something of a tradition lives on.

The luxurious **Fullerton Bay Hotel** offers stunning views and a rooftop landscaped pool and rooftop bar. The hotel also operates the old Customs House which has been transformed into a dining and entertainment complex.

Further south, it is worthwhile to leave the waterfront and visit **Lau Pa Sat** (18 Raffles Quay) which means 'old market'. This was a wet market during the colonial days but today, it is a food centre that has retained its old charm and its original architecture. It is a temple to Singapore cuisine and Victorian architecture. It has recently been renovated back to its old 'Glory' using the original 3000 cast iron pieces brought in from Europe, and has become very popular again.

*Lau Pa Sat*

Lau Pa Sat has food from all over Asia but it is famous for its satay stalls, many of which are behind the main centre. The chefs are enveloped in sparks and smoke as they fan their coals with large palm leaves. It is hot, tiring work which might explain why many of these satay stalls have operators who are very aggressive. Inside it is quite calm. This is one of only a few hawker centers that remain open 24 hours

Back on the waterfront, the **Marina Bay Financial Centre** is a large mixed-use development on Marina Boulevard consisting of three office towers, two residential towers and the retail Marina Bay Link Mall. The new Downtown MRT station is connected to the basement of the mall.

If you are not in need of retail therapy, you should walk along the paved and landscaped promenade which forms a key pedestrian link between the developments at Clifford Pier and the Marina Bay Sands. Midway along here is the **Marina Bay City Gallery** (https://www.marina-bay.sg/marinabaycitygallery.html) where you can learn the story behind the Marina Bay development.

This is the sister gallery of the Singapore City Gallery in the Chinatown area. Visit the Marina Bay City Gallery to understand more about the amazing urban transformation of Singapore's new extended downtown. The two-storey building with sustainable design features has plans, information on the technological advances that have been pioneered here, and events at Marina Bay. Admission is free but it is closed on Mondays.

The huge **Marina Bay Sands** (www.marinabaysands.com/) is said to be 'the world's most expensive building' but the developers have got quite a complex for their money. The unique building has transformed Singapore's skyline and added a major tourist attraction since it opened in 2010.

The **Marina Bay Sands Hotel** has three 55-story towers with 2,561 luxury rooms and suites. Across the top of the towers is the Sands **SkyPark**, which houses restaurants, gardens, a spectacular vanishing edge pool, and a public cantilevered observation deck. Most of the area is reserved for hotel guests but the observation deck is open to the public from 10 a.m. to 10 p.m. for a current cost of S$23 for adults, S$17 for children and S$20 for senior citizens.

The Sands Expo and Convention Centre, Marina Bay Sands Casino and The Shoppes at Marina Bay Sands are all connected to the hotel towers. Visitors should bring their passports to show that they are foreign citizens as locals have to pay an entry fee to enter the 24-hour casino which is spread over several floors. There is also a dress code prohibiting beachwear and other very casual attire.

**The Shoppes at Marina Bay Sands** (www.marinabaysands.com/shopping.html) with its canal with gondolas, two Crystal Pavilions, an indoor skating rink and the MasterCard Theatres have become a must-visit place for visitors to Singapore for good reason. The development is huge and quite stunning.

*Marina Bay Sands Hotel*

The Event Plaza at The Shoppes is a great place to enjoy the nightly **Wonder Full** show, (www.marinabaysands.com/entertainment/wonderfull.html) a 13-minute light and water show featuring lasers, lights, and other effects. It is set to a 140-piece orchestral soundtrack and tells about the journey of life.

The show is visible from both sides of the water. If you are standing in front of the hotel looking towards the city you can hear the music and see the projected images on the water fountains. Bubble machines create a shimmering cloud above your head and you can see the impressive images of Singaporean children projected onto the wall of water.

From the city side looking towards the hotel you see not only the water fountains but also a series of lasers which light up Marina Bay Sands and the ArtScience Museum.

Out the back of the hotel is the free and very impressive **Gardens by the Bay**, (www.gardensbythebay.com.sg/) a 100 hectare park consisting of several waterfront gardens. In my opinion the best time to visit here is late afternoon or early evening as it can be too hot during the day to fully appreciate this wonderful place. This also allows you to visit the SkyPark observation deck near sunset, which again is the best time to see this attraction.

Don't miss the conservatory complex which comprises two cooled conservatories – the Flower Dome and the Cloud Forest, despite the admission charge. The conservatories provide an all-weather education-entertainment space within the Gardens. Both are around 1 hectare (2.5 acres) in size and the Flower Dome is claimed to be the world's largest column-less glasshouse. They provide a nice break from Singapore's hot and humid atmosphere.

The Cloud Forest houses a seven storey tall mini-mountain ecosystem. There is a waterfall, which serves to cool down the ambient temperature. Take the meandering path around the base of the mountain before hopping on the elevator to the 6th storey. A staircase then leads to the highest reaches of the mountain. Here, a beautiful water feature abounds with plant life.

From here winding walkways, which are set in positions that allow you to view the ecosystem from multiple perspectives, lead downwards. Along the way there are excellent views of the external features of Gardens by the Bay, such as the Supertrees and the Flower Dome.

The Supertrees are tree-like structures with heights that range to 50 meters (160 ft). They are vertical gardens and there is an elevated walkway between two of the larger ones providing an aerial view of the gardens. At night, the Supertrees perform a 15-minute free light and music show called the OCBC Garden Rhapsody which culminates when the trees seem to explode in a firework-like fashion. Show times are 7.45 p.m. and 8.45 p.m.

Elsewhere there is an adventure trail consists of trampolines, balancing beams, hanging bridges and much more and a Children's Garden which is a water playground. The children will get totally wet but it is good for cooling them down and there are change rooms for getting into dry clothes after the visit. At the Heritage Gardens you can learn how plants play a part in the culture of Singapore's main ethnic groups. There are numerous restaurants and cafes in the gardens

Just outside the gardens is the **Marina Barrage** (www.pub.gov.sg/marina) which was opened in 2008 and now provides water storage, flood control and recreation opportunities. The Barrage is a 360 m long dam built across the Marina Channel to keep out seawater. The resulting reservoir supplies Singapore with 10% of its water needs. It and its control building have proved to be a tourist attraction and it is open for viewing 24/7.

There is an information counter which is open from 9 a.m. to 9 p.m. daily. The Marina Barrage draws visitors from around the world to visit the sustainability exhibits and use the green roof of the control building for popular activities, such as kite flying and picnicking.

As a lasting physical legacy of Singapore's Jubilee year, **Jubilee Walk** was launched late in 2015. It covers historic locations in the civic district and the Marina Bay area, and starts at the National Museum of Singapore and ends at the Marina Barrage.

Further south, the **Marina Bay Cruise Centre** (http://mbccs.com.sg/) is a new terminal located next to the Marina South Pier. Also near here is the **Singapore Maritime Gallery** (http://maritimegallery.sg/) where you can learn how Singapore transformed itself into one of the world's leading international maritime centers.

It opens 9 a.m. to 5.30 p.m. except for Mondays and admission is free. This whole Marina South area is still being developed and will become a major sporting and development area in years to come.

Back on the Marina Bay foreshore the **ArtScience Museum,** (www.marinabaysands.com/museum.html) in a building said to resemble a lotus flower, is the next attraction. The permanent exhibition consists of three galleries - Curiosity, Inspiration, and Expression. Permanent exhibits include objects showing the accomplishments of both the arts and the sciences through the ages but these are often secondary to visiting exhibitions.

The Museum says it "seeks to understand what drives creative people, how they acquire and use their skills, and how the world around us is changed because of it". It opens daily from 10:00 a.m. to 7:00 p.m.

We now walk across the **Helix Bridge**. It has four viewing platforms which provide excellent views of the Singapore skyline and events taking place within Marina Bay. The bridge has a distinctive double helix structure modeled on the structure of DNA and is 2890 m long.

The bridge leads to **Youth Olympic Park,** (https://www.nparks.gov.sg/gardens-parks.../parks.../youth-olympic-park) an art park located on Raffles Avenue. This is named after the inaugural Youth Olympic Games which were held in Singapore in 2010. There is a landscaped maze with a 4.5-metre high "mountain". There is also a rock wall featuring 18 drawings by youths which depict some of Singapore's most famous icons, and Olympic-themed art pieces.

The **Singapore Flyer** (30 Raffles Avenue) (http://www.singaporeflyer.com/) is a giant Ferris observation wheel with 28 air-conditioned capsules capable of holding 28 passengers which opened in 2008 across the expressway from the park. It is interesting to note that after operating for some months the wheel's travel direction was reversed for feng shui reasons.

The Flyer has an overall height of 165 meters (541 ft) and is the second tallest in the world. A trip lasts approximately 32 minutes.

Apart from the basic ride, there are other options. You can choose to have high-tea, champagne or a four-course meal while you are onboard the Flyer. Journey of Dreams is a multimedia showcase that provides a deeper appreciation and understanding of the Singapore Story and the Singapore Flyer. Occupying the entire central atrium of the main Terminal Building, is a rainforest where you can take a relaxing stroll along the 5 winding access paths after your experience on board Singapore Flyer.

Back on the Marina, **The Float @ Marina Bay** is the world's largest floating stadium. It has been the venue for the annual National Day Parade (Singapore National Day is 9 August) and was used for the Opening and Closing Ceremonies of the Singapore Youth Olympic

Games. The adjacent Seating Gallery has a capacity for 30,000 spectators and is used during the Grand Prix which is usually held in late September.

*Singapore Flyer*

Immediately west from here is the popular **Makansutra Gluttons Bay**, (http://www.makansutra.com/eateries-home.aspx?mid=1) an outdoor food centre with a nice outlook across the bay. This is a good place to try Fried Hokkien Mee, Oyster Omelette, Carrot Cake and BBQ Chicken Wings. They are all very good.

The centre is used by both tourists and locals and while prices may be a little higher than in some other hawker centers, it makes up for that with its convenience. There is a good view of the music and light show which originates from the Sands complex every evening.

Continue walking around the marina on the Waterfront Promenade until you reach the unusual-shaped **Esplanade – Theatres on the Bay**, (https://www.esplanade.com/) a purpose-built centre for performing arts. It contains a Concert Hall and a 2000-seat Theatre. The unusual design is said to look like a durian fruit.

There are often free concerts here on the bay-side open air stage. The rooftop is accessible and the view is excellent. It is accessed from the top floor next to the library entrance.

The complex contains many nice restaurants and bars and right next door is the Makansutra Food Centre (or Glutton Bay) which is one of the best out-door eating places in the area.

Across Raffles Avenue are three of Singapore's prime hotels - Mandarin Oriental, Marina Mandarin and the Ritz Carlton - and **Marina Square**, (www.marinasquare.com.sg/) a shopping mall filled with a range of medium to high-end fashion boutiques, restaurants and lifestyle shops. There are stores like Zara, John Little, and Marks & Spencer, and over 250 shops. For entertainment there are the Golden Village Cinemas and a ten-pin bowling alley.

Further north is the Pan Pacific Hotel and the Conrad Centennial Hotel. These are surrounded by the **Millenia Walk** shopping centre (www.milleniawalk.com/) and the **CityLink Mall**. There is certainly no shortage of shopping opportunities in this area!

Finally we reach **Suntec City** (www.sunteccity.com.sg/) with its five buildings and convention centre. A highlight here is the bronze **Fountain of Wealth** where the balance of metal and water supposedly paves the way for success. It has a music and laser show in the evening.

The **Suntec City Mall** was the largest shopping centre in Singapore until the opening of VivoCity in 2006. There are 300 retail outlets, 50 pushcarts and 100 food and beverage establishments spread across 4 floors and 4 zones. We have reached the end of our walk and both the Promenade (CC4/DT15) and Esplanade MRT (CC3) stations are within easy walking distance.

# 5 ORCHARD AND HOLLAND ROADS

**Orchard Road** is a two kilometer-long shopping street that is a huge tourist attraction. Any serious shopper is destined to spend much time here in the most popular shopping enclave in town. Orchard Road acquired its name from the orchards and plantations that were here in the mid-1800s. Today you can peruse a bevy of shopping malls, conveniently stacked one after the other along both sides of the street and a few is adjacent areas.

While this is certainly shopping central, the area has some other attractions that will be of interest to those less inclined to max out the credit card. We will start our tour at Dhoby Ghaut MRT station (CC1/NE6/NS24) the largest MRT interchange in Singapore, and work west from here. This was named after the Hindi term for Indian laundrymen who went door to door to collect clothes to wash.

It is quite a way to our final destination but there are plenty of buses along our route that can be taken if the feet get too sore. Shady trees line the road between malls providing some relief from the sun.

**Plaza Singapura** (68 Orchard Road) (www.plazasingapura.com.sg/) is directly above Dhoby Ghaut MRT and there is a direct connection from the station. This urban mall with its emphasis on fashion, entertainment and food for families and young adults has retail outlets spread over nine floors. It is Singapore's oldest air-conditioned shopping mall but has recently been given a thorough facelift. There is a huge Carrefour multilevel hypermarket, numerous eating options and a large cinema complex on the top floors.

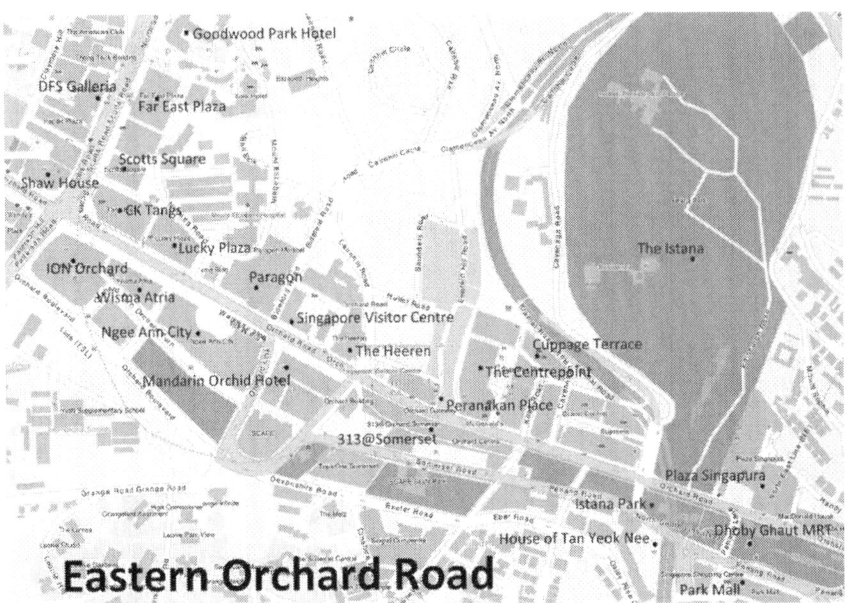


If we had taken another exit we could have gone across the small park to **Park Mall** (Penang Road) (www.parkmall.com.sg/). It is not one of the larger malls but it is strong on quality. There are more than 70 stores over five levels dedicated to fine furniture, lifestyle items, and the latest homeware designs from leading brands. It also features a European-style internal shopping street, modeled after London's Burlington Arcade.

While on this side of Orchard Road you should look at **The House of Tan Yeok Nee** on the corner of Clemenceau Avenue, once the mansion of a successful 19th-century Chinese merchant, which is now home to a branch of the University of Chicago business school. Surrounded by high walls, it has two courtyards and the imposing entrance hall would have been the ancestral room and reception hall.

**Istana Park** (https://www.nparks.gov.sg/gardens-parks-and.../parks-and.../istana-park) is directly in front now. Its identifying landmark is the

Festival Arch, a concrete and stainless steel structure rising from a rectangular pool. Dwarf coconut palm trees are planted within small pools making the trees look like they are growing in the water. The small park has a nice range of foliage, a popular cafe, and is beautifully lit at night.

**The Istana** (http://www.istana.gov.sg/the-istana/open-house/visitors-information-0), on the north side of Orchard Road was completed in 1869, and was once the Government House of the colony of Singapore, before becoming the official residence and office of the President after independence. The building has elements of Indian and British architecture but the cross-shaped plan is similar to a traditional Malay palace.

The 40 hectare grounds have several gardens and even a 9-hole golf course but they are only open to the public on five days a year. There is a changing of the guard ceremony every first Sunday of the month at around 5.45 p.m.

## Going West along Orchard Road

The Concorde Hotel and Shopping Mall is immediately west of the Istana. The mall on the lower two floors of the complex is not one of the more attractive centers along here. The OG Orchard Point lifts the standard a bit with the five level OG department store providing a wide range of products.

Cuppage Road, which is named after the first owner of this area, runs between Orchard Point and Centrepoint. It contains **Cuppage Terrace**, a strip of restored shophouses now housing bars and restaurants, which is worth a short detour.

After a revamp in 2006 **The Centrepoint** (176 Orchard Rd) (http://thecentrepoint.frasercentrepointmalls.com/) emerged from the 1983 Centrepoint shopping centre and now it is being revamped again after losing several of its major tenants.

The mall will remain open during the renovation which is scheduled to be completed in the second half of 2016. The mall contains a Metro store and clothing retailer Gap amongst others. It is a popular family mall due to some extent to the active promotion of its 'in-mall' activities.

Across the road from here are some other malls and the Somerset MRT station (NS23). **Orchard Central** (181 Orchard Rd) (www.orchardcentral.com.sg/) is a modern, twelve-storey mall with outdoor escalators and nice views from the terraces. Fronted by an iconic exterior featuring an eye-catching digital art membrane, the mall has a cluster concept, grouping complementary offerings together to serve as special destinations for shoppers.

There are several floors devoted to food, what is claimed to be the world's tallest indoor climbing wall, a nice collection of public art, and a 24/7 Roof Garden and Discovery Walk.

**Orchard Gateway** is a new mall which is part of an integrated development which includes a hotel and office tower. It provides an overhead bridge across Orchard Road. There is nothing that particularly draws you here except for the very modern Library@Orchard which opened late 2014. This is worth a visit for anyone who is interested in what a modern library can look like.

**313@Somerset** (313 Orchard Road) (www.313somerset.com.sg/) is right next door and is directly linked to the Somerset MRT station. There are four floors of mid-range local and global fashion labels including Zara, Uniqlo, and Esprit and some popular dining options. In addition there are three basement levels with direct access to Somerset MRT station.

Back on the north side of Orchard Road again is **Peranakan Place (www.**peranakanplace.com/home/) which has historic colonnaded covered walkways and there are some nice, cosy places to sit and relax including a shaded terrace cafe with lots of potted foliage.

Just beyond this you can see some lovely restored Chinese style terrace houses along Emerald Hill Road with their carved dark timber half-doors, polished tiles and mirrors to ward off evil spirits. These are some of the most expensive homes in the city.

The **Singapore Visitor Centre** (www.yoursingapore.com/en.html) at 216 Orchard Road is an essential stopping point if you missed the outlets at Changi Airport. You can make enquiries about attractions, pick up some maps and brochures, make hotel reservations, book tours and buy attraction tickets.

Back across on the southern side of the road is the popular movie-set themed **Cathay Cineleisure**, (www.cineleisure.com.sg/) a complex of cinemas, shopping and cafes attracting mostly a young crowd. There is also a popular karaoke chain and e-gaming centre. The building has won awards for its creative colors.

Next door the highly popular Mandarin Orchard Hotel has the four-level **Mandarin Gallery** (333 Orchard Road) (www.mandaringallery.com.sg ) with some one-of-a-kind specialty stores and boutique eateries. This is a smaller mall than most and the ambiance is more sedate.

The **Heeren** (www.heeren.com.sg/) is another complex that has recently been renovated. Most of the commercial building is taken up by the large Robinsons department store which runs over six floors. This is a home-grown Singapore department store with an illustrious history as a trusted retailer.

After crossing Orchard Link, the standard of some of the malls picks up further. **Paragon** (290 Orchard Rd) (www.paragon.com.sg/) has long been one of Singapore's flashiest malls, packed with luxury brands in 200 stores and six levels. There is a food market in the basement, and cafés on most floors. Paragon offers high-end browsing with style, space and, of course cold air-conditioning.

There are also three department stores in the complex – Metro, Marks and Spencer and Muji. Paragon Medical, a medical tower that hosts specialist clinics in cosmetic surgery, dentistry, radiology, obstetrics, and traditional Chinese medicine helps set this apart from other malls.

**Lucky Plaza** (304 Orchard Road) (www.luckyplaza.com.sg/) is not up-market. There are some camera and electronics stores on the ground level, cheap souvenirs on the second floor, low cost salons on the fourth floor and a cheap, good food court in the basement. You might be lucky and get shopping bargains, especially for electronic goods such as cameras, tablets, and DVD players. You will see many Filipino domestic workers here on Sundays.

**CK Tangs** (320 Orchard Road) (www.tangs.com.sg) is Singapore's very own department store in a lovely Chinese-style building. As the first retail store on Orchard Road in 1958, Tangs started the transformation of this area into what it is today. The store is strong on women's fashion with several iconic brands and there is an excellent basement food area worth visiting.

Across the road are three other substantial developments. **Ngee Ann City/Takashimaya Shopping Centre** (391 Orchard Road) (www.ngeeanncity.com.sg/) has expensive branded goods above ground and more affordable shopping in the two basement levels. With its imposing façade and grandiose interiors, it is a popular stopover for some shoppers for a couple of hours. The two hand-carved dogs that guard the main entrance were imported from China to bring prosperity.

The huge Takashimaya Department Store offers a choice of fashion and accessories for adults and children, enrichment centers, hair and beauty salons, health stores and pharmacies, restaurants and bars, and even a fitness club.

Kinokuniya, south-east Asia's largest English-language bookstore, is on the 3rd floor while there are many food outlets selling fare from all around the world. A post office, ticket booking office, banks and a health club help make this a complete centre. The indoor Takashimaya Square comes alive with regular bazaars and fairs that draw shoppers and others while the outdoor semi-circular Civic Plaza has been a venue for many prestigious events.

**Wisma Atria** (435 Orchard Road) (www.wismaonline.com/) is an unusually designed mall with boutiques and international brands across five levels. The centre offers over 100 specialty stores anchored by leading Japanese department store Isetan, fashion brands GAP and Nike, and foodies Food Republic. There are also two aquariums and a wide array of fine dining restaurants. It is linked underground to

Orchard MRT station (NS22) and neighboring malls.

**ION Orchard** (2 Orchard Turn) (www.ionorchard.com/) is the largest and flashiest new shopping mall with 330 stores including Cartier, Louis Vuitton, Prada, Dior, DKNY, Giorgio Armani, Burberry, Calvin Klein, and Dolce & Gabbana. There are also more affordable options including Japanese retailers Uniqlo and Muji. The extensive and popular food hall offers visitors myriad food choices and the fourth floor ION Art gallery is a nice addition to this part of the city.

ION Sky, located on levels 55 and 56 of the tower building, houses an observatory, bar and contemporary restaurant called Salt Grill. You buy tickets for the observatory from the concierge counter on level 4 of the shopping mall. As at January 2016 the trip was free between 3 p.m. and 5.30 p.m. There is a Singapore Visitors Centre on level 1.

Before we continue along Orchard Road, a detour up Scotts Road is worthwhile. Passing the Singapore Marriott Hotel we reach **Scotts Square** ( 6 Scotts Road) (www.scottssquareretail.com/). The art pieces by artists such as Salvador Dali and Henry Moore, and the stunning Victoria & Albert Museum chandelier, immediately set it apart from other shopping malls.

Although this is smaller than many of the malls it makes up for this with quality shops and restaurants. The 40 levels above the mall are occupied by up-market apartments.

The Grand Hyatt Hotel is next to Scotts Square, then you come to **Far East Plaza** (14 Scotts Road) (www.fareastplaza.com.sg/) which has been a bargain hunter's paradise but it is slowly creeping up-market. It is still good for unique clothes and accessories at reasonable prices.

There are hundreds of small shops run by individual small traders such as jewelers, sporting goods outlets, souvenir shops, banks and money changers, travel agencies, a supermarket and so on. Bargaining here is a 'must'.

While here walk a little further north to the **Goodwood Park Hotel** (www.goodwoodparkhotel.com/) with its turrets and decorated facade set in lovely gardens. This started life in 1900 as a German Club, was seized by the government when World War I started, then became a hotel in 1929 and was one of the most famous in south-east Asia. During World War 2, it was the headquarters of the Japanese army but returned to being a prestige hotel in 1947 and it remains so today.

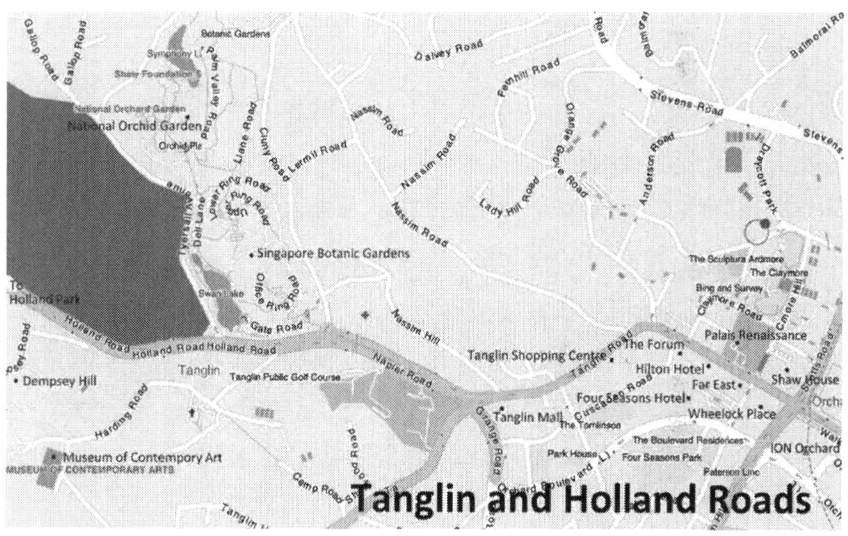


Back across Scotts Road is **DFS Galleria Scottswalk** (25 Scotts Road) (http://www.dfs.com/en/tgalleria-singapore) a multi level mall that features mostly upscale fashion brands and on the lower floor, cosmetics. This is not a traditional shopping mall, however, as DFS is the well known duty free chain that caters almost exclusively to international travelers.

Show your passport for duty-free savings on international luxury brands like Burberry, Mont Blanc, Dunhill, Prada and Tiffany & Co. There is a global guarantee on all purchases but in my experience prices are not significantly lower than elsewhere.

At the corner of Orchard Road is **Shaw House and Shaw Centre** (350 Orchard Road) (https://en.wikipedia.org/wiki/Shaw_House_and_Centre). This houses the main store of Isetan in Singapore and it has a Japanese supermarket in the basement. The building also houses a total of 11 cinemas including one featuring Singapore's first and only IMAX's Digital Theatre System. The recently renovated Shaw Centre with a large range of eating places is connected to Shaw House.

Moving west, there are plenty of other centers. **Wheelock Place** (501 Orchard Road) (www.wheelockplace.com/) has seven levels of retail outlets in its glass-covered cone, the well-known British department store Marks & Spencer with fashion, foodstuff, and toiletries on the ground floor, and there is a pretty good selection of restaurants on the 2nd floor. The mall has an underpass to Shaw House and ION Orchard.

**Far East Shopping Centre** (545 Orchard Rd) (www.fareast-plaza.com/) is a rather old and complex centre with jewelry and precious stones, computers, health equipment, tailors and beauty shops. There are also several bars and restaurants. Some like it because it is so different to the new fancy malls.

**Hilton Hotel and shopping centre** (581 Orchard Road) (www.hiltonshoppinggallery.com/) is up-market with designer labels including Gucci, Donna Karan, Giorgio Armani, Missoni, Paul Smith and Louis Vuitton. The Four Seasons Hotel with its *Vitality* sensuous bronze sculpture is behind here on Orchard Boulevard.

The **Forum Shopping Mall** (583 Orchard Road) (www.forumtheshoppingmall.com.sg/) is next. This has a mix of retail stores and eateries. There is an emphasis on children with the likes of Toys R Us, Kids 21 and Guess Kids, and there are also a pediatric clinic, speech and drama centre, children's hair salon and nutrition centre. Parents will find international labels like Emporio Armani, Tsumori Chisato and Club 21b.

On the north side of Orchard Road opposite the Hilton Hotel is **Palais Renaissance** (390 Orchard Road) (http://www.palais.sg/about.php) a small, exclusive shopping destination with an assembly of exclusive boutiques. DKNY, Gucci and Steinway Pianos are here.

As the road curves south it changes name to Tanglin Road but the shopping experience continues. The four-storey **Tanglin Shopping Centre** (19 Tanglin Road) is packed with exotic regional artifacts, antiques, artwork and jewelry. It also has fashionable fabrics and furniture from across south-east Asia. The mall also caters for fans of classic vintage items such as old movies and DVDs, books and retro fashion.

### Tanglin, Napier and Holland Roads

The final mall along here is **Tanglin Mall** (163 Tanglin Road) (www.tanglinmall.com.sg/). With its colonial and tropical architecture, this is an older style niche mall for the expatriates, yuppies & professionals. Outlets cover fine dining to fashion and home decor and there is a supermarket, pharmacy and food court in the basement. The mall hosts flea markets regularly on Saturdays.

It is somewhat a relief to come to Napier Road and know that we have left the shopper's paradise. Things even get better when we reach the **Singapore Botanic Gardens** (https://www.sbg.org.sg/) (enter via the Tanglin Gate with its four trademark pillars and the supporting swinging gates). The Gardens began in 1859 and have been developed and expanded continuously since then. It has been instrumental in developing the rubber tree industry and pioneering orchid hybridization.

The gardens have been approved as a UNESCO World Heritage Site. This is the first listing for Singapore and it is only the third botanic garden to be so recognized. It opens from 5 a.m. to 12 midnight every day of the year, and there is no admission fee.

There are three cores: Tanglin which retains the charms of the historic Gardens; Central is the tourist belt of the Gardens; and Bukit Timah the educational and discovery zone. Each has its own appeal so it is well worth devoting several hours for your visit. Volunteers run free guided tours of parts of the gardens every Saturday morning. Call 6471-7361 for further details.

The Gardens has a small tropical rainforest, an Evolution Garden showing how plants evolved on Earth, a one-hectare Ginger Garden, the Jacob Ballas Children's Garden, three lakes and several statues, a

Healing Garden and the **National Orchid Garden** (https://www.nparks.gov.sg/gardens-parks.../national-orchid-garden).

Since 1859, orchids have been closely associated with the Singapore Botanic Gardens and now the Orchid Garden has over 1000 species and 2000 hybrids on display. This is the largest display of orchids in the world. The splendor of the sweeping floralscape is quite stunning. The Orchid Garden is the only place within the gardens with an admission charge but I assure you it is well worth while. The gardens are stunning and have the largest display of orchids in the world.

Some of the highlights of the Orchid Gardens are the Tan Hoon Siang Mist House, the Cool House which encloses a representation of high elevation tropical sites, the Celebrity Orchid Garden, the VIP Orchid Garden and the Orchidarium. You can also see Singapore's national flower, the VANDA Miss Joaquim. I urge you not to miss visiting here.

Eateries within the garden include Blue Bali, Bliss Kidz Cafe, Casa Verde in the Visitor's centre, Food for Thought at the Botany Centre, Food Canopy by the Nassim Gate, The Dunearn which serves contemporary Western fusion cuisine and offers a la carte and set menus to diners and Halia Restaurant, at the Ginger Garden.

Halia is particularly special at night when it is lit by discreet lamps and soft moonlight. There are also gift shops available.

Children under 12 can do puzzles, learn about food that comes from plants, play in the fountain play area and the sandpit, climb the tree-house, cross a swinging suspension bridge, enter the cave behind the waterfall and explore the maze within the Children's Garden. Admission is free but adults must be accompanied by children if they wish to enter. Entry is from Bukit Timah Road at the northern end of the gardens.

Once you have had your fill of the gardens, it is not far along Holland Road to **Dempsey Hill** (www.dempseyhill.com/). This has become one of the city's top lifestyle destinations. It boasts a hip cluster of wining and dining establishments, set amid quiet surroundings within conserved colonial black-and-white buildings.

Dempsey used to be the site of the British army barracks in colonial times and it was where young men reported for military service in the early 1970s. Now there are specialty food purveyors and restaurants, art galleries, antique furniture stores, Asian-inspired clothes, a fitness centre and weekend farmers markets on Saturdays every few weeks.

In the evening (and this is the best time to visit) you are able to satisfy every craving with Indian curry houses next to European eateries, local seafood establishments, a great Jim Thompson Thai restaurant, a microbrewery, fusion and more. Note that at times taxis can be difficult to come by here.

Close by you will find the new **Museum of Contemporary Art** (27A Loewen Road) (http://www.mocaloewen.sg/), an integrated arts facility that presents works not normally carried by the national museums in Singapore. It opens 10 a.m. – 6 p.m. daily and there is a nice cafe.

Nearby **Holland Village** is a favorite haunt for the expatriate community in Singapore and for a growing number of university students. It exudes a laidback charm and is a good place to relax while listening to music. Prices used to be high but since the students have been frequenting some of the outlets, some prices have come down to 'Singapore normal'.

There is an array of shopping and entertainment options where there are live music joints, ritzy restaurants, coffee houses and casual wine bars together with a wet market (selling fresh meat and fish) and antique stores. The local food court is popular and many of the food outlets open late into the evening.

It is just a short walk to the Holland Park MRT station (CC21).

Another place worth visiting in this general area is **Pasarbella @ the Grandstand**, (200 Turf Club Road, Bukit Timah). Unfortunately it is too far to walk from Holland Park so you will need to take a taxi. PasarBella claims to be an amalgamation of the quirky and rustic interiors of Covent Garden in London, and the rich aromatic scents of fresh, organic produce in Melbourne's Queen Victoria Market. In many ways it succeeds.

As a premium grocery shopping destination, PasarBella stocks a wide range of both local and international brands in over 30 stores that provide products that are extremely niche and exotic in nature. To add to the ambience, live music and busking performances keep both the young and old entertained. It opens daily from 10 a.m. to 9 p.m.

In other parts of the Grandstand you will find some excellent restaurants. For seafood you could try Ah Yat Seafood Restaurant and Owen Seafood Restaurant while others include Tunglok Xihe Peking Duck, Modern Asian Diner and The Ascot.

# 6 KAMPONG GLAM AND LITTLE INDIA

These two areas provide a colourful and aromatic journey through Singapore's past. Kampong Glam was the location of the palace of Sultan Hussein, the Malay leader who ceded the island to Raffles. Little India began as a camp for Indian convict workers who were brought in by the British to work on the city's development. Both areas still have important religious centers and are hubs for traditional businesses which many visitors find fascinating.

We start at Bugis MRT station (EW12/DT14) which is in a district just outside this area but is worth seeing in its own right.

In the mid 20th century, **Bugis Street** was renowned for its flamboyantly dressed transvestites and as the most notorious red-light area in Singapore. In the evening, the entire street would become a market offering a wide selection of cheap goods, hawker food, and sex. This has now gone and the area has become a collection of buildings and malls mainly catering to young locals.

The Singapore Tourist Promotion Board has jumped on to the bandwagon and now bills it as "the largest street-shopping location in Singapore". The largest complex is **Bugis Junction Mall** (200 Victoria Street) (www.bugisjunction-mall.com.sg/), part traditional mall, part open-air shopping district, which has sidewalk cafes, shophouses and new retail places side by side.

*Bugis area*

There are glass-covered, air-conditioned shopping streets amidst a nostalgic architectural setting. From Straits Chinese-style facades to shop houses with five-foot walkways, Bugis Junction exudes a touch of historical charm while serving the needs of the modern shopper. The shops and sidewalk cafes, have an old town atmosphere but they can get very crowded at times.

There is a fountain in the middle of Bugis Square and a four-storey building above the MRT station. The five-star InterContinental Hotel is also part of the complex. The basement has a good selection of eateries, and there is a Food Junction food court on the 3rd level. There is a cinema complex on the fourth floor. The shoppers here are mostly young people so many shops sell trendy fashions, accessories, shoes, bags, dining, etc.

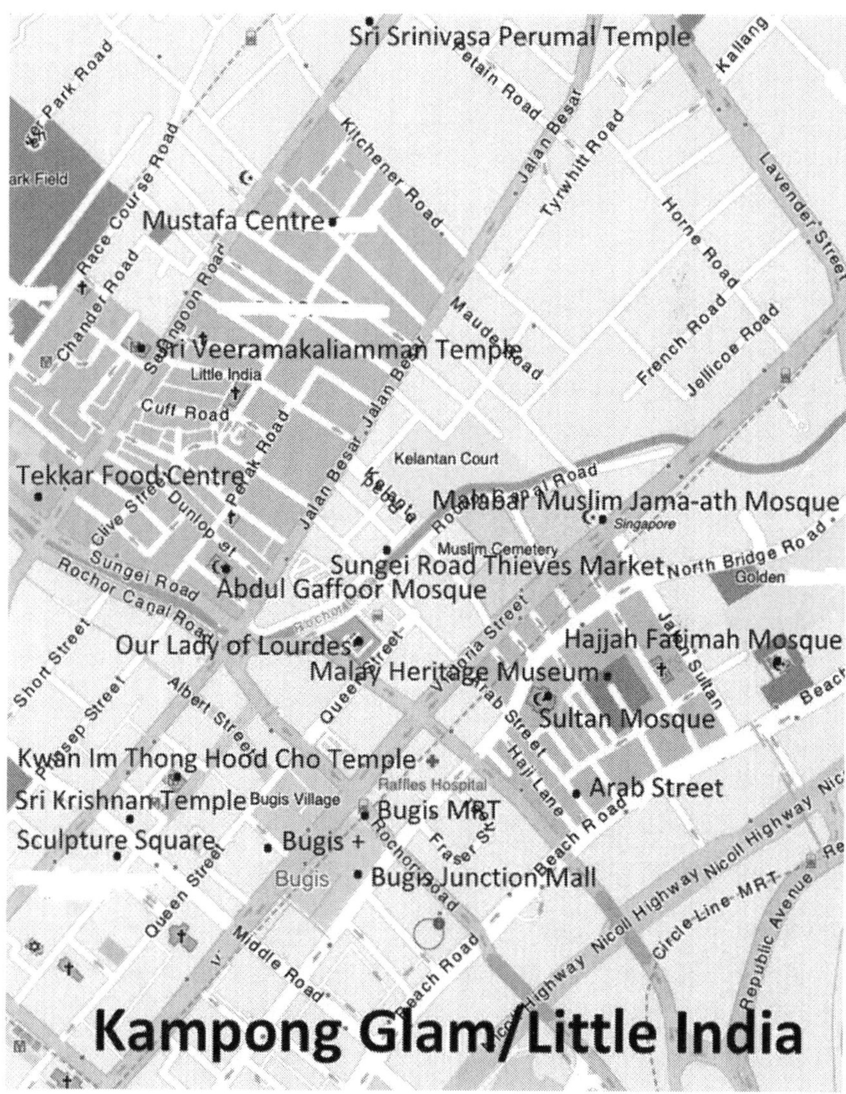


Across Victoria Street is Bugis+, a 10 storey shopping mall which has the largest Uniglo store in Singapore, and is connected to Bugus Junction by an above-ground walkway. It has become a familiar landmark with its illuminated "crystal" façade. Also here is the crowded Bugis Village, a hive of stalls selling clothes, shoes and accessories, plus a few manicurists and nail bars, and food stalls. Don't expect much quality, but it can be fun to shop here.

On the other side of Bugis+ and Bugis Village is Queen Street where there are several hotels and a couple of churches. These don’t hold any particular interest but if you go one more street to the west there are several attractions.

The **Kwan Im Thong Hood Cho Temple** (178 Waterloo Street) is a traditional Chinese temple that has existed here since 1884 although it was extensively rebuilt in the early 1980s. The entrance has a large gateway flanked by two smaller gates. Note the many medicine sellers and fortune tellers that congregate around here. The temple is dedicated to Kuan Yin, the Goddess of Mercy who some say can grant wishes, which may help explain why it's always packed.

To have your wish come true, you need to remove your shoes, join a line, light several joss sticks, make a wish then place the sticks in the urns provided. You then pick up the container filled with wooden sticks and shake it until one of the numbered falls out. You take the number to an interpretation office and receive a paper with your general fortune and an indication of whether your wish will come true. Good luck!! No photography is permitted inside the temple.

Close by at No 52 is the **Sri Krishnan Temple**. This is a South Indian Hindu temple dedicated to Sri Krishna and his consort Rukmini, but it draws many other visitors. The Sri Krishnan Temple was established in 1870 on this site when an idol of Sri Krishna was set up under a banyan tree.

The present building, with the large statues of Hanuman and Garuda guarding the entrance, is impressive. Note the statues which adorn the entrance spire and remove your shoes before entering. To take photographs inside there is a fee. The complex is much bigger than it looks.

At the corner of Waterloo Street and Middle Road is another attraction. **Sculpture Square** (155 Middle Rd) has been created in buildings originally built in 1870. The Chapel Gallery was formerly a Baba Methodist Church and is one of the few remaining Gothic style buildings in Singapore. Sculpture Square is an art space dedicated to the promotion, and development of contemporary 3-dimensional art.

Next to the Chapel Gallery lies the Gallery Block. This was once a mission hostel but it now hosts exhibitions of contemporary and small sculptures. This is also a good place to pick up a bite to eat from Artichoke, a café that serves simple food using its own fresh cheese, butter, pickles, condiments, sausages, cured meats and fish, or from Overdoughs, a takeaway bakeshop and deli.

We are now going to the Kampong Glam area so walk along Middle Road to North Bridge Road and turn north. You will have passed the **Singapore Design Centre** which has been established in the 120-year old premises of the former St Anthony's Convent. You can drop by the Centre to view a furniture exhibition or attend a seminar on how design can transform a business or whatever happens to be on at that time.

*kapok*, an offshoot of the Hong Kong-based cult lifestyle and design boutique, is located on the ground floor for shopping and a cafe.

Along North Bridge Road you will find Parkview Square on your right after crossing Rochor Road. This building dominates the skyline and the area and it is surely one of the world's greatest Art Deco buildings. The forecourt is great with statues of the world's greatest thinkers and others (Lincoln, Churchill, Beethoven, etc.), and you are free to walk inside and snap away.

It is a working office building upstairs, and there is security, but they don't mind you getting a few photos. The ground floor bar is sensational and you need to stop for a drink. One of the unique attractions is an angel that flies up into the atrium to retrieve wine and champagne from cool storage.

**Kampong Glam**

You are now approaching Kampong Glam, a historic district whose name originates from the Gelam Tree, which once grew abundantly here and was used in building ships. Rows of brightly painted shophouses line several streets, and many of them are occupied by trendy design firms, restaurants, art galleries, and craft and curios shops.

*Haji Lane*

We cross Ophir Road then turn left into either **Haji Lane** or **Arab Street** which is where Singapore's early Arab traders settled, and the part of town allocated to the Malays by Raffles. It was the centre of the original Muslim section of town, famed for its specialty shops, Muslim restaurants and more. There are many backpacker hostels in this area.

Tiny Haji Lane, hidden away in the heart of the Muslim quarter, is a fashionista's paradise. The collection of narrow shop-houses has in recent times been transformed into an aggressively hip retail stretch with something in common with New York's Meatpacking District. There is great architecture for photographers and it is excellent for art and vintage shoppers.

While perhaps it is not visually stunning to most, this area has vibrant color and is a great place to explore slowly. There are textile stores and outlets selling Persian carpets and you'll also see leather, perfumes, spices, jewelry, crystal and baskets for sale. It's easy to spend a couple of hours visiting many of the stores and chatting with the sellers. Quality seems good and prices, once you bargain, are OK too.

One of the more unusual places here is Selfie Coffee Singapore (11 Haji Lane) where you can get a coffee with your photograph on top in the foam. It is an interesting concept and the coffee and cakes are quite good.

Look for the Muslim restaurants, the money-changers and the travel agents who specialize in the travel needs of Muslim pilgrims heading for Mecca. Stop off at a coffee house or browse for traditional games such as Congkak which involves marbles and a wooden board. It is a place to observe and move slowly.

Back on Beach Road the **Hajjah Fatimah Mosque** (4001 Beach Rd) is worth seeing. The mosque was built in 1846 and is an unusual mix of local Islamic and Western architecture which gives it particular appeal to visitors. It is enclosed by a high wall, and the compound has a prayer hall, a mausoleum, Iman quarters, an ablution area, and a garden.

It has a distinctive minaret which some say is a copy of the original spire of St. Andrew's Cathedral. The mosque is skewed from the street to face Mecca, and it has a large onion dome.

*Malay Cultural Centre*

A highlight of this area is the **Malay Cultural Centre** (85 Sultan Gate) (www.malayheritage.org.sg/), a place which is very important to Malay Singaporeans. The building was once the Istana Kampong Glam or Sultan's Palace, which was housed in a much larger compound than we see today.

The lovely much reduced grounds, which are free, stay open until 8 p.m. Here you can see Gelam trees, a replica of a Bugis boat, a fountain, and information markers on the history of the Bugis people.

The building houses the **Malay Heritage Museum**, which preserves and showcases the Malay culture and heritage in Singapore. The ground floor shows the importance of Malays in the trading culture of

Singapore while upstairs there are displays on aspects of the Malay community. It has a rich showcase of Malay heritage and culture in Singapore, with historical artifacts, interactive multimedia and colourful exhibits from Singapore's national collection as well as contributions from the community.

The museum costs S$4 adults, S$2 seniors and students to visit and is open Tuesday to Sunday from 10 a.m. to 6 p.m. The rooms are a bit bare, and frankly it is not overly exciting for international visitors but the cost won't break the bank.

Go a few streets to the north-west of here to the **Malabar Muslim Jama-ath Mosque** (corner of Victoria Street and Jalan Sultan), the only Malabar Muslim mosque in the city. It was completed in 1963 as a traditional mosque in layout and general form. The main prayer hall which is surrounded by open galleries on three sides is elevated by one storey and is oriented towards Mecca. There is a separate two-story annex and an octagonal tower which is capped by an onion dome.

It's a matter of retracing our steps to North Bridge Road and then travelling south to the **Sultan Mosque** (3 Muscat St) (www.sultanmosque.sg/), one of the most important mosques in Singapore. A mosque was first built here in 1826 with a grant from the British East India Company and the present building was completed in 1928 to a fairly simple design with Moorish overtones by an Irish architect.

It is not particularly spectacular but the gold dome has appeal and there is a carpet that was donated by a prince of Saudi Arabia. The main hall can accommodate 5000 worshipers. If you wish to enter and are not dressed appropriately there are cloaks available free of charge.

During the fasting month of Ramadan, Kampong Glam is a great place to experience Muslim culture and festivities. The best time to visit is at 'breaking of fast' in the evenings when Muscat Street comes alive with a bustling night markets set up during this period.

We leave Kampong Glam here and head towards nearby Little India. Walking west along Arab Street, you will notice **Our Lady of Lourdes** (50 Ophir Road) (www.lourdes.sg/ ) off to the left. This neo-Gothic church with fine details opened in 1888 and is said to have been modeled on a church in Lourdes, France.

Outside the white paint, tall spire and rose window are impressive while inside there is a grotto with statues depicting the Lourdes 'miracle'. Note the floor which is tiled in a geometric pattern using blue, cream, brown and white tiles. Masses are held here in English, Tamil and Singhalese.

## Little India

A complete contrast is provided by the **Sungei Road Thieves Market** which was once one of the most popular flea markets in Singapore, but you may be disappointed. There are quite a few vendors selling mainly junk and the present site which is affected by road and MRT work has no ambience whatsoever. The market has been here since the 1930s and it's been a real shopping institution in Singapore but it is scheduled to shut down in 2017.

Back in the old days, it was the place to go to buy stolen goods but today, most of the items are probably legitimate. To me it seems a rather sad place with some very poor people selling stuff that most people don't want to buy. You now enter Little India, a place that becomes very crowded on the weekend.

You are now in Little India proper, one of Singapore's most vibrant districts. As you walk down Serangoon Road and neighboring streets, explore their mix of Hindu and Chinese temples, mosques and churches. Enjoy the South Indian vegetarian food, North Indian tandoori dishes and local fare like *roti prata* (round pancakes) and *teh tarik* (pulled tea in Malay) the sweet, milky beverage that is poured at a height from one container into another to aerate it and give it its distinctively frothy top.

To the west, the small but charming **Abdul Gaffoor Mosque** (41 Dunlop Street) was constructed in 1907, and major restoration of the building was completed in 2003. The main entrance has an elaborate pediment, the centre of which is a sundial. The prayer hall is raised above the ground and is surrounded by verandas. It is oriented towards Mecca and thus skewed from the street. An information centre can provide robes for those not appropriately dressed.

There are some interesting old buildings and intriguing shops to see as we move further south-west. Take your time to immerse yourself in the color, smell and culture before arriving at the **Tekka Food Centre and Market** (665 Buffalo Road). This is a landmark in Little India and is part wet market, part food centre and part shopping mall.

Thirty years or so ago, vendors operated in the street from mobile barrows. For reasons of hygiene, the government banned this, licensed them and provided formalized markets such as Tekka.

The centre is used by Chinese vendors, Indian stall owners and Malay retailers, and it sells a huge range of products. There are stalls selling South and North Indian food, Chinese dishes and Malay cuisine. You will be eating with the locals and with short-term workers from India and Bangladesh. Since there are many stalls and they sell similar food, there is huge competition between them.

The somewhat challenging wet market downstairs sells fresh seafood, fruits, and vegetables, some of which have been flown in from Sri Lanka and India. The whole place becomes very crowded on weekends so it is probably better to avoid it at that time.

When you're done exploring the market, exit to Serangoon Road and cross the street to find the **Little India Arcade**. This cluster of 1920s shophouses has been given conservation status and contains dozens of shops selling everything Indian. It's a great place to find small trinkets, Indian CDs, and traditional Indian clothing or you could try the Indian sweets from Moghul Sweet Shop.

**Serangoon Road** which runs beside the market is a wonderful place to wander. There are small restaurants, endless shops and great street scenes to observe. You should try some of the very traditional and economical Indian food and also some of the teas.

You will find a great range of Indian sari cloths which make good wall hangings if you don't want to wear them and the metal Tiffin sets can be useful and good gifts. This area gets very crowded on a Sunday when immigrant Indian and Bangladeshi laborers descend here en mass.

Just off Serangoon Road at 5 Campbell Lane is the new (mid 2015) **Indian Heritage Centre** (http://www.nhb.gov.sg/institutions/indian-heritage-centre). This is the first museum in south-east Asia to focus on the diverse heritage of the Indian community. The four-storey architectural gem comprises permanent galleries featuring five themes, a special exhibition gallery, as well as educational and activity spaces that provide a good learning experience for all visitors.

The galleries span the period from the 1st century to the 21st century. Visitors can learn about the historical links between the Indian sub-continent and south-east Asia, as well as the experiences of South Asians in south-east Asia. The Centre is closed on Mondays. There is free admission for locals while foreigners pay S$4 adults and S$2 seniors and students.

Almost opposite Campbell Lane is Buffalo Street aptly named because this area used to have buffalo holding pens and a slaughterhouse. Towards the end of Buffalo Road turn right on tiny Chander Road. On the corner, at 37 Kerbau Road, you will see an historic house built in 1900 by a Chinese businessman which was restored in 1990 by the government. It is a great example of a house owned by wealthy Chinese.

Almost directly across the street on Chander, you'll see the **Shree Lakshminarayan Temple**. This Hindu temple with its red domes is dedicated to the incarnation of the goddess Kali. Go north on Chander to Belilios Road and turn right. If you're hungry for Indian food there are many options around here.

The **Sri Veeramakaliamman Temple** (141 Serangoon Road) (www.sriveeramakaliamman.com/), which is dedicated to the ferocious Hindu Goddess of power Kali, is central to Little India. The temple was built by Tamil laborers from southern India in a style familiar to them. Devotees ring the tiny bells that cover the temple doors, before entering, so that their requests can be answered by the gods.

Inside, the air-conditioned sanctum area has well-decorated walls and ceilings while there is a jet black statue of Kali, flanked by her sons in the main shrine. Also here is an altar with nine statues representing nine planets. Locals circle the altar and pray to their planet for help when they have a problem.

Photography is permitted inside the temple, please just remember to be respectful of people who are there to worship. The new six-storey annex building in the temple compound houses several facilities including a wedding hall and several dining halls.

Further north is the **Mustafa Centre** (145 Syed Alwi Road) (http://www.mustafa.com.sg/). This is the place to go if you need a new TV, gold jewelry, new cooking pot or some underwear at 4 a.m. because this place never closes. It has a cult following, is usually crowded, constricted , cramped , confusing and crazily chaotic but is one of the best places to go if you're after a bargain.

It is not fancy but it has a great range of items (300,000 the store claims), and generally good prices to match. Some visitors complain about the slackness of the staff and prices for some things are higher than in the markets but it really is a shopping experience unlike any other particularly after midnight. Mustafa Centre has what are claimed to be the best money-changers in Singapore and its own travel agency.

Desker Road a narrow side street is named after the first English butcher in Singapore, but as anyone who has seen it after dark will know, it's now famous for its cheap, licensed brothels.

Going north, you pass the popular Parkroyal on Kitchener Road Hotel before arriving at the **Sri Srinivasa Perumal Temple** (397 Serangoon Road). This large complex, dedicated to Vishnu, dates from the 19$^{th}$ century, but the 20-meter-tall Gopuram, or monumental tower, was built one hundred years later. At the main door, statuary stands guard on either side of the large wooden door.

Inside the main temple you will find blue statues of Perumal, his consorts, and his bird-mount, the mythical Garuda. Look up and see the ceiling which is dominated by a colourful pattern depicting the nine planets of the universe. There are several subsidiary shrines dedicated to different deities. As with all temples you should wear suitable conservative clothing and remove your shoes if you wish to enter the temple.

This is the temple where the Thaipusam (usually held late January) procession starts on its way to the Chettiar Temple over three kilometers away on Tank Road. You have probably seen photographs of the Devotees with hooks and spears into their flesh. The festival is both to give thanks for good luck, and to pay penance for "sins" committed during the past year.

We are right at the northern extreme of Little India now but there are two further places worth visiting. The **Sakya Muni Buddha Gaya Temple** (336 Racecourse Road) is one of the most prominent and widely visited Buddhist temples in Singapore. It was founded in 1927 by a Thai monk and there is a 15-meter high statue of a seated Buddha, as well as many smaller Buddha images and murals.

The statue is surrounded by a stylized aura made from numerous light bulbs so it is often referred to as the Temple of 1,000 Lights. This can appear somewhat tacky to Western visitors but it is all taken seriously by the local devotees. At the base of the statue is a fresco depicting important events in Buddha's life. Before leaving, go into the small room beneath the altar to see an image of a reclining Buddha.

The name Racecourse Road comes from when nearby Farrer Park was once a sports field with an oval and Singapore's first horseracing track. On non-racing days, it became a golf course, but the presence of grazing buffaloes caused much annoyance. It was also where the first airplanes landed in Singapore; but the length of the park was too short for them to take off again so they had to be pulled into Serangoon Road which was not much more than a dirt track at the time.

The **Leong San See Temple** (371 Racecourse Road) is an incense-filled Taoist Buddhist temple with fearsome-looking dragons on its exterior. The temple resembles an ancient Chinese Palace, and is dedicated to the Goddess of Mercy. There are very intricate designs lining the walls and pillars.

Inside, the main altar is dedicated to Kuan Yin and is framed by beautiful, ornate carvings of flowers, a phoenix, and other birds. To the right is an image of Confucius where parents bring their children to pray for intelligence. Behind is an ancestral hall dedicated to the deceased.

Along Race Course Road, Banana Leaf Apolo is popular for South Indian food. Try the famous local delicacy, fish head curry. Walking south from here we end up at Farrer Park MRT station (NE8).

Little India, like several other areas in Singapore, has several tours offered by various operators. One such operator is The Diverse-City Trails (http://trails.thethoughtcollective.com.sg/), a partnership between The Thought Collective and Ben & Jerry's designed to create a shared experience among participants and spark two-way discussions around the issues Singapore faces. There are currently three trails operating from March to November.

The Little India Trail is designed as an intimate yet sobering exploration of the Little India community. It shows how larger economic and social forces have transformed how this community lives. This trail looks into into the broader challenges Singapore faces in light of urban development, space management and community conservation.

One of Singapore's oldest housing estates, Toa Payoh was once Singapore's test bed for various social innovations to build cohesion amongst communities. You will be shown how happy neighbors in a community are forged and explore the way forward.

Another operator is Journeys (http://www.journeys.com.sg/singaporewalks/tours_dhobis.asp). To do this tour you meet at Little India MRT Station, outside Exit E (Buffalo Road) on a Wednesday at 9.30am. The tour finishes at 12.00noon. The tour visits The Paan and Garland store, Tekka Wet Market, Little India Arcade, the Sri Veeramakaliamman Temple and elsewhere.

Summer Footprints Pte Ltd. (http://www.etour-singapore.com/little-india-walking-tour.html) walking tours are run on Tuesday and Friday, departing at 9.30 a.m. and ending about 12.30 p.m. The Meeting Point is the Little India MRT Station (Exit C).

# 7 SENTOSA AND THE SOUTHERN ISLANDS

**Sentosa** is a popular island just south of Singapore, visited by some twenty million people a year. It was first developed about 40 years ago but was often a disappointment to international visitors. Now it is coming into its own and I suggest that it is a 'must-visit' place to see for all visitors. There are now sufficient offerings of interest to adults and children to keep everyone amused for a day or two.

Some of the attractions are a 2 km long sheltered beach, Fort Siloso, golf courses, a range of accommodation options, numerous small activity centers, the highlights of Resorts World Sentosa, and Universal Studios Singapore.

Before going to the island, however, there are a few mainland attractions that we should see. We will start our exploring at the Harbourfront MRT station (CC29/NE1). This is located within **VivoCity** (www.vivocity.com.sg/), Singapore's largest shopping mall. There are numerous stores, a huge hypermarket, two giant food courts with a good selection of outlets, and some landscaped areas. It would be easy to spend all day here.

Visitors will notice the art collection by 6 international artists displayed all around VivoCity. If you are exploring the complex it's not easy to miss the rooftop water feature in Sky Park spanning the area of 4 Olympic-sized swimming pools, which has become an icon within VivoCity. Also worth checking out is the rooftop amphitheatre which offers a platform to showcase the vibrant arts and cultural scene in Singapore.

The Singapore Cruise Centre is connected to VivoCity via a bridge to the **HarbourFront Centre** (1 Maritime Square) (www.harbourfrontcentre.com.sg/), another shopping mall and ferry terminal that has boats that connect to nearby Indonesian islands. The 3-story retail destination, offers everything from fashion, food & beverage to sporting equipment, electronic goods and more.

To the west are several office buildings which are connected to the mall and the Sentosa Cable Car station is housed in HarbourFront Tower 2. This is a cable station between Sentosa Island and Mt Faber.

**Mount Faber Park** (https://www.nparks.gov.sg/gardens-parks-and-nature/parks-and-nature-reserves/mount-faber-park) is a popular tourist destination and one of the oldest parks in Singapore. The 100 m tall hill has look-out points which offer a panoramic view of Singapore while a mural wall depicting scenes of local history can be seen at Upper Faber Point, the highest point in the park.

The hill is covered by secondary rain forest and there are walking trails through the wooded areas and some splendid colonial-era black-and-white bungalows. If you get this far don't miss the interesting Henderson Waves, the highest pedestrian bridge in Singapore, which is frequently visited for its artistic, distinctive wave-like structure consisting of a series of undulating curved 'ribs'.

It joins Mount Faber with adjoining Telok Blangah Hill and you can continue to walk through a chain of small parks across the Alexandra Arches to the Kent Ridge Canopy. This is called the **Southern Ridges Walk**. The total distance is about nine kilometers and it is not an easy stroll but for nature lovers it is worthwhile. There are some shelters with drinking fountains and toilets along the way.

One of these small parks is Hort Park. Here you will find tranquility away from the urban buzz of Singapore. The Butterfly Garden, Lifestyle Corner and the Flora walk are some of the highlights of this 23-hectare park. There is a collection of well manicured and well designed gardens and you can picnic on the lawns or a enjoy glass of wine at the bistro on the grounds. The park holds regular events throughout the year and you can join guided tours or attend workshops and talks.

Mount Faber Park has a good selection of food and beverage outlets such as Faber Bistro and further dining options are available at Faber Peak which houses a retail shop, the cable car station and restaurants and bars. This was constructed with the cable car to Sentosa Island in 1974.

The current cable car cost (February 2016) is $29 (Adult) and $18 (Child) for foreigners and while this seems high there is no disputing the fabulous view you get on the ride across to the island. This price also includes the new cable car on Sentosa Island itself.

The other attraction for some will be St James Power Station, a music and nightlife venue with multiple nightclubs and live entertainment destinations. When built in 1926, it was Singapore's first coal-fired electricity power plant.

There are basically four ways to reach Sentosa Island, the cable car from Mount Faber or Harbourside, the Sentosa Express light rail from VivoCity, the footbridge from near VivoCity, or a taxi from anywhere within Singapore.

Sentosa could be reached by ferry when a terminal opened on the island in 1987 but this was demolished in 2007. The causeway bridge was opened in 1992 allowing traffic and pedestrians to access the island. The Sentosa Express commenced operations in 2007 and the Sentosa Boardwalk opened in 2011. My preference is to walk one way and take the Sentosa Express the other way.

Your exploration of the island will be governed by which you do first. If you walk, you will start exploring from the north and finish at the south. If you take the Express, I suggest you go to the last station and work north from there. It also depends on what you want to see. Universal Studios and Resorts World are in the north, while the beaches and the nightly Wings of Time are in the south.

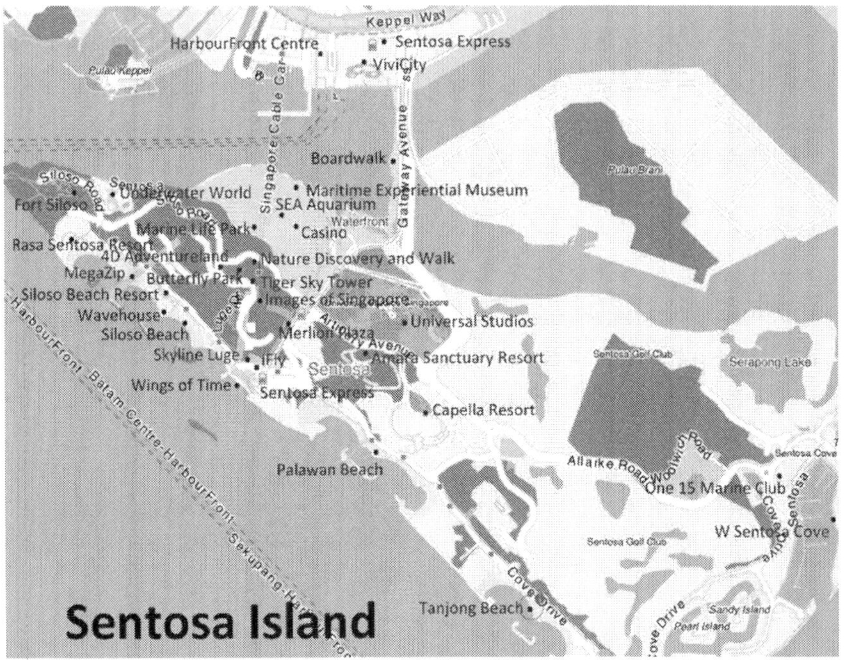


The Sentosa Boardwalk takes about 15 minutes to traverse and there are gardens, shops and eateries along the way. It can be hot during the day but there are two-way canopy-covered travellators to help. There are some good views from here particularly in the evening. It normally costs S$1 to cross but for all of 2016 it is free.

The Sentosa Express light rail station is on the 3rd floor of VivoCity beside the large food court. You need to buy a ticket which currently costs S$4. The train operates every 5-8 minutes from 7 a.m. to 11:45 p.m. daily. Once on the island you can walk to many of the attractions but there are also three bus routes and one beach tram route to help you reach some of the more distant attractions.

An intra-island cable car opened in June 2015. You can journey over the jungle, sand and sea on the new Sentosa Line which will take you to dozens of attractions on Sentosa. There are three stations: the Merlion station, Imbiah Lookout station and Siloso Point station.

There is no logical way of seeing all of Sentosa's attractions so I will just comment on them as we circle the island. Let's start at the Imbiah Lookout area which is at the end of the cable car from Singapore island.

The **Tiger Sky Tower** (www.skytower.com.sg/) is a free-standing observation tower providing a panoramic view of Sentosa and the Southern Islands. On a clear day, you can also see the nearer parts of

Malaysia and Indonesia. Unlike most observation towers you don't take elevators or stairs to reach the sightseeing point. Here it comes to you.

You enter a 72 person air-conditioned cabin at ground level and it then revolves slowly as it climbs to the top of the tower. The trip take about 10 minutes and the cost is S$18 adults and S$10 children.

The **Butterfly Park and Insect Kingdom** (www.jungle.com.sg/) is a nearby landscaped garden with live butterflies, exotic insects and some birds and animals. It is housed in a cool outdoor conservatory, and there are several buildings with exhibits. Whether the admission price of S$16 is good value for you will depend on your interest in butterflies and insects. I must say it has limited appeal to me.

The **Sentosa Nature Discovery and Nature Walk** (http://www.sentosa.com.sg/en/nature/sentosa-nature-discovery/) consists of an indoor information gallery, at the start of the trail and then an elevated nature trail that connects with a series of hiking trails that meander through the hills. It is a free attraction and is a delight on a day when a breeze makes walking enjoyable.

There are eight different types of habitat found on Sentosa, including some of the rarest: coastal rainforests, rocky seashores and wetlands.

**Sentosa 4D Adventureland** (www.4dadventureland.com.sg/) is an interactive movie experience with 4-dimensional digital effects. During the movie you will be tossed about in your seat, feel the wind blowing in your face and experience other effects. There is also the Desperados, a 4D interactive shoot-out game where you can aim for the top Sheriff honor, and the 4D simulation Exteme Log Ride at the same location.

Many will like to follow the misadventures of Captain Lucky and his band of pirates in search of hidden treasure. A One-Day Adventure Pass Including unlimited entries to- Journey 2, Extreme Log Ride, Desperados, and Interactive 4D Shoot-Out Game is S$ 38.90 Adult, S$ 26.90 Child. A Single Ride on "Pirates" is S$20.90 Adult, SS20.90 Child.

I think **Images of Singapore LIVE** in conjunction with **Madame Tussauds** is one of the better attractions in this area since it was completely remodeled in mid-2015. It would need to be with an admission price of S$39 adults, S$30 seniors, and S$29 children.

It is an historical museum with exhibits showing the history of Singapore using multi-media displays, multi-screen theatre presentations and more together with the excitement usually associated with Madame Tussauds displays.

Visitors are led by actors through fifteen new highly immersive areas which weaves together Singapore's story. These areas include a quayside walk, Malay fishing village, Commercial Square, Jubilee Cinema, television shop and others. The final leg of the journey involves going onboard The Spirit of Singapore, a boat ride that uses dynamic lighting and multi-sensory effects.

Visitors can photograph and pose with their favorite A-listers such as Angelina Jolie and Brad Pitt, challenge sports stars, hop on stage with music legends such as Lady Gaga and come face to face with international icons from Singapore, Asia and beyond.

There are several food outlets In the Imbiah Lookout area including Starbucks, The Arches and Tastes of Singapore. Both bus 1 and 2 and the new cable car connect this area to other parts of the island but I suggest you ride the escalators down to **Merlion Plaza** and its Imbiah Sentosa Express station. The centre-point here is a 37-meter tall replica of the Merlion complete with viewing galleries and a souvenir shop. Admission to the Merlion is S$12 / Adult, S$9 / Senior Citizen / Child.

Merlion Plaza forms a north-south axis through the island. The northern end leads to the Festive Terrace while in the south a winding walkway leads to the Central Beach Plaza and Beach Station. This is the end of the Sentosa Express light rail system and is a transfer hub for the bus and beach tram services. There are also three worthwhile attractions here.

**Skyline Luge Sentosa and Skyride** (http://www.skylineluge.com/luge-singapore/skyline-luge-sentosa/) is part go-cart and part toboggan. The non-motorized cart allows the rider to speed 650 m down a hill towards the beach. To reach the top, there is the Skyride that offers a panoramic view of the coastline. This is an attraction suitable for both adults and older children. Three rides on the Skyride and Luge are S$25 per person.

**iFly** (http://www.iflysingapore.com/main.html) is for the real adventure seekers. It provides the thrill of skydiving without the jumping, plunging and airplanes. Participants receive training and guidance from certified instructors before the actual skydive experience. At S$109 for two rides it is not cheap but it is a very unique experience.

The third attraction is now called **Wings of Time** (www.wingsoftime.com.sg/) but many will know it as Songs of the Sea which ran in this location for six years. It features dancing water fountains, enhanced pyrotechnic effects and a live cast. You view the performance from a large open-air viewing gallery. The 25-minute show runs twice nightly every evening at a cost of Premium Seats S$23 / person and Standard Seats S$18.

The beach stretches both east and west from here and you can walk in either direction. There is also a free beach tram that operates along here and this is very useful in hot conditions. Tanjong Beach and Palawan Beach are to the east. **Tanjong Beach** is popular for its tranquility and solitude. The sand is clear, the water at times less so. The Tanjong Beach Club offers seafood from around the globe, tropical fruit cocktails, beach volleyball, a pool and entertainment at night.

Family-friendly **Palawan Beach** has good sand and interesting shops and eateries. There are wading pools and water fountains for kids to cool off in, an aviary and the Animal & Bird Encounters show. A suspension bridge links to the Southernmost Point of Continental Asia, a small islet with a viewing deck at the top of the towers which are located there.

**Port of Lost Wonder** at Palawan Beach is Singapore's first kids' club by the Beach. Designed to provide a unique experience of family bonding, the attraction houses a signature water play area, themed islets for picnics and leisure activities and distinctive retail and dining experiences for the very young and young at heart. Admission is weekdays S $10/ child, school holidays, weekends & public holidays S$15/ child, adults are free.

A major new attraction is set to open here May 2016. **KidZania Singapore** will be an indoor family edutainment centre which offers an interactive learning and entertainment experience for kids in a kid-sized city, through over 80 role-play activities. More than an indoor theme park, kids will be able to experience role-play activities, earn a salary in the form of kidZos, the official currency of KidZania, pay for goods and services and manage a bank card.

**MOSH!**, located just above Kidzania at Level 3, is Singapore's first digital media edutainment facility which allows visitors to create imaginary worlds of their own in an immersive virtual environment. Admission charges are Adult - S$28, Child - S$22.

Long **Siloso Beach** stretches to the west of Beach Station. This is claimed to be Singapore's hippest beach, and on weekends it is alive with people day and night. There are bars, you can surf a man-made wave at **Wavehouse Sentosa** (www.wavehousesentosa.com/) and there is a whirlpool bath on the beach. There are several shopping options, the Bikini Bar, and bistros and restaurants.

Siloso has free volleyball courts available on a first-come-first-served basis and you can try skim-boarding, kayaking, cycling, and rollerblading. The **Flying Trapeze** is something quite different. It offers fun and excitement for visitors– whether you're participating or lust watching.

You can learn to soar high above the beach and get your timing just right to enjoy a smooth mid-air transition and a burst of applause. It only opens in the afternoon and admission is S$10 per swing, or S$20 for 3 swings.

The **MegaZip Adventure Park** (www.megazip.com.sg/) has a range of attractions other than the 450 metre Zip-line which travels 75 meters above ground level at speeds of up to 60 km/h, across the jungle, the beach, and the sea.

These include a high-rope adventure course, a simulated parachute jump, a super trampoline, and a 16 meter-high climbing wall. Each attraction can be entered by itself while there are combination packages for adventure freaks. MegaZip cost S$39 / zip, Climbmax is S$39 for 24 obstacles, ParaJump is S$19 / Jump while NorthFace is S$19 / 20 mins.

Shangri-La's Rasa Sentosa Resort and Spa is at the end of the beach and behind this is **Fort Siloso**. This was built by the British in 1880s to protect the western approaches to Singapore and is now open to visitors. There are various guns from past times, models depicting fort activities and an exhibition with photographs, and films. Items are spread over quite an area and it's quite hilly so you can get quite hot while moving around.

The 11-storey (181 meters) Skywalk trail provides guests a scenic trek among the treetops en route to Fort Siloso. Note the lift operation hours are 9 a.m. to 7 p.m. Admission to the Fort is free and the cost of the Surrender Chambers is S$6 / Adult, S$4.50 / Senior Citizen / Child.

**Combat Skirmish LIVE** allows you to enjoy a session of Combat Skirmish in a Historical War Fortification. You can navigate through an indoor maze, shoot down your opponents, dodge their attacks and achieve specific team missions. Alternatively you can battle against mechanical soldiers through the 1st Tunnel Battle in Singapore.

**Underwater World and Dolphin Lagoon** (http://www.underwaterworld.com.sg/) is an oceanarium which opened in 1991. At that time it was one of the best in the world but now it is somewhat dated. There are supposedly more than 2,500 marine creatures here including stingrays, moray eels, turtles, sharks, and seals. There are various programs such as 'Dive-with-the-Sharks' on offer. Admission is S$29.90.

The Underwater World also includes a Dolphin Lagoon where there are several daily shows of varying quality. Again various programs are on offer including "Meet-the-Dolphins" sessions which allows you to closely interact with the dolphins. A more expensive "Swim-with-the-Dolphins" program is also available.

We now finally come to the **Resorts World Sentosa** precinct and this has added a number of further attractions to the island. The first seems to be a direct competitor to Underwater World.

**Marine Life Park** is claimed to be the world's largest oceanarium. It consists of two major attractions and provides an opportunity for close encounters with animals of the marine world. **S.E.A. Aquarium** (http://www.rwsentosa.com/language/en-US/Homepage/Attractions/SEAAquarium) is currently the world's largest aquarium with more than 100,000 marine animals from over 800 species. A one-day pass currently costs S$32/ Adult, S$22/ Child (4 - 12 years old) and Senior Citizen.

This also includes admission to the innovative **Maritime Experiential Museum** where you can experience Singapore's past as a trading port. There are artifacts from the Bakau shipwreck and the Temasek archaeological site and you can view life-sized ship replicas of Asian sailing vessels from the docks at the Historic Ship Harbour. The visit ends in the 360 degree multimedia Typhoon Theatre where you 'board' a sailing ship and encounter a perilous storm.

Marine Life Park's **Dolphin Island** offers a range of programs that gives you the opportunity to interact with Indo-Pacific Bottlenose dolphins and to learn about them. Hopefully this will inspire visitors to a deeper understanding of marine life, and to discover more about dolphins. Programs start at around S$70.

A further component is the **Adventure Cove Waterpark** (http://www.rwsentosa.com/language/en-US/Homepage/Attractions/AdventureCoveWaterpark), a tropical paradise of waterslides and an epic journey along Adventure River. You can snorkel with 20,000 colourful reef fish and wade with dozens of rays. One day passes currently cost S$36/ Adult, S$26/ Child and Senior Citizens.

Then there is the **Trick Eye Museum** (www.trickeye.com/singapore) which refers to an art technique that turns two-dimensional paintings into three-dimensional images through the use of optical illusions. 2D paintings on the museum walls, floors and ceilings appear to pop out of the surface and come to life. The museum consists of six zones - 'World of Masterpiece', 'Safari Kingdom', 'Star of Circus', 'Dream of Fairy Tale', 'Love In Winter' and 'Adventure Discovery'.

You can step inside the paintings to make a story with your camera. There are a total of 90 artworks. Fortunately they only allow a certain number of people in at any one time so it doesn't get too crowded. A one-day pass costs S$25 adults and S$20 for children and seniors.

There are two free shows that you should see. **Lake of Dreams** is a spectacular choreographed display of fire, water and light with a musical score. There are flaming dragons, water cannons, and laser special effects, all in a spectacular show. It is presented every night at 9.30 p.m. at Festive Walk.

**Crane Dance** is produced each night at 9.00 p.m. at the Waterfront using the world's largest pair of animatronic cranes in a multimedia spectacle of lights, sound, water jets and pyrotechnic effects. The combination of audio visual technologies and stunning light and water effects tells a love story that can be appreciated by all.

The **casino** is also free to overseas guests but you need to show your passport. It is hidden away underground beneath the Crockfords Tower hotel. There are hundreds of gaming tables offering 19 different games. A dress code applies which prohibits such things as slippers, singlets and shorts and you must be 21 years or older to enter.

This finally brings us to what has become Sentosa's biggest attraction. **Universal Studios Singapore** (http://www.rwsentosa.com/Homepage/Attractions/UniversalStudiosSingapore ) has cutting-edge rides, shows, and attractions, most of which are based on films and television series.

There are seven zones around a lagoon all with roller coasters or other movie-themed attractions such as TRANSFORMERS The Ride, Shrek 4-D Adventure, Madagascar: A Crate Adventure, and Jurassic Park Rapids Adventure. You can purchase your day passes online and save time queuing when you arrive at the park. A one day pass costs S$74 for adults and S$54 for children.

On weekends the park can get quite crowded so arriving early is a smart move. Normal operating hours are 10 a.m. to 7 p.m. but they do vary throughout the year so check the web site.

The Sentosa Waterfront Food Hall is located outside near the main entrance to Universal Studios. It is a recreation of street side eating in a nice air-conditioned atmosphere with considerable choice of food at reasonable prices.

Some visitors decide that Sentosa Island is a good place to stay and there is a wide range of **accommodation** to choose from. The Club at Capella Singapore with 81 serviced apartments, penthouses and manors is considered one of the best and its parent the Capella Singapore, situated in lush grounds, is also superb.

Most of the hotels that are part of Resorts World are five-star properties. They include Crockfords Tower, Hotel Michael, Hard Rock Hotel Singapore, Festive Hotel, Equarius Hotel, and Beach Villas. All are considered to be good but which one will appeal to you will be determined by the style of property you most enjoy.

Elsewhere Shangri-La's Rasa Sentosa Resort is a beachfront five-star hotel with 454 rooms and suites. The Amara Sanctuary Resort Sentosa has 121 rooms. Siloso Beach Resort has 194 units overlooking the sea. The Sentosa Resort & Spa is another five-star hotel with 214 rooms and suites set in nice grounds. Perched on a hill overlooking Siloso Beach,

Costa Sands Resort (Sentosa) has 34 Deluxe Rooms and 15 *Kampung* (Malay for 'village') huts that accommodate 4 guests overlooking Siloso Beach. This cheaper resort has a swimming pool, barbecue pits and a café.

Sofitel Singapore Sentosa Resort & Spa is the newest French luxury 5-star hotel in Sentosa offering a haven of tranquility and relaxation. The 215-room hotel has several eating areas, lounge, indoor & outdoor event spaces, spacious swimming pool , So SPA services, high-tech gym facility, and kids playroom.,

Mövenpick Heritage Hotel Sentosa has 5-star rooms in a Contemporary Wing, or the Heritage Wing, The glass covered link-bridge spanning across the two wings of the hotel is home to Galleria, where you can savor a taste of English and local High Tea. Tablescape, the all-day dining restaurant, serves buffet breakfast, signature Western delights and local favorites.

The W Singapore Sentosa Cove is a 240-room five star luxury resort hotel at the Quayside on the eastern side of the island. The ONE 15 Marina Club Singapore is also located here.

The other **southern islands** have little development and much less appeal to those seeking action. They can, however, be havens for those seeking tranquility in an otherwise frenetic city. The major southern islands for visitors other than Sentosa are Kusu Island, Lazarus Island, Palau Seringat, Pulau Hantu, Pulau Tekukor, Saint John's Island, and the two Sisters' Islands.

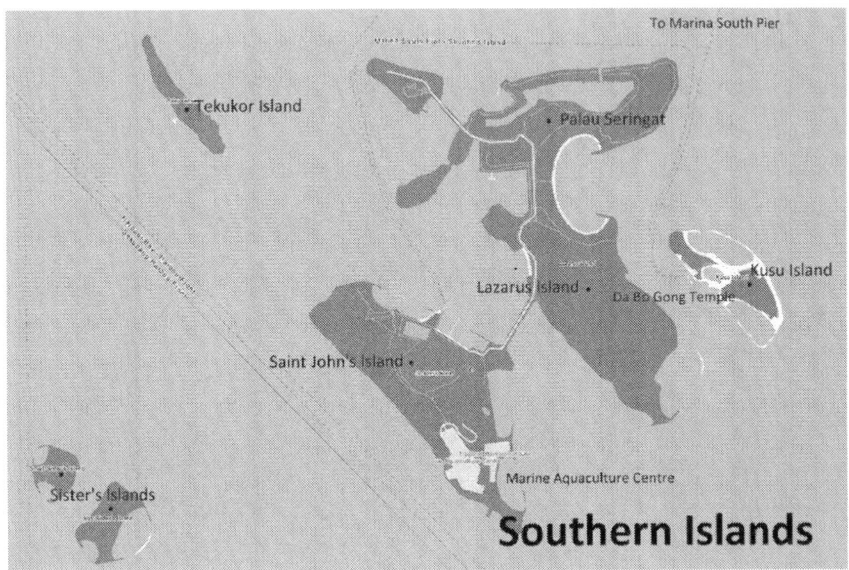


Land reclamation has linked Pulau Seringat and Lazarus Island and a causeway has been built to connect Lazarus Island and Saint John's Island. Water-based activities are the attraction and a wide variety of corals can be found in the waters surrounding the islands but visibility is not always good.

You may be able to see giant clam, seahorses and octopus. Overnight camping is only allowed on Sisters' Island and Pulau Hantu with permits available from the Executive, Southern Islands Management, Sentosa.

Ferries run to two of the islands from the ferry terminal at Marina South Pier in the Marina Bay precinct. A round-trip ferry ticket to St. John's Island then on to Kusu Island and back, costs S$18 (adult) and S$12 (child). The one-way journey takes about 30 minutes.

It is probably best to visit the islands on Sundays and public holidays as there are more ferries and they operate till later compared to other days. The islands are favorite spots for anglers chasing selars, tambans, groupers, squid, and so on.

**Saint John's Island** was the site of Sir Stamford Raffles' anchorage before meeting the Malay chief of Singapore in 1819. The island was used as a quarantine station in the late 19th-century then later as a jail and drug rehab centre.

Today, the island has tranquil greens for picnics, trekking routes, soccer fields, and saltwater lagoons for swimming. There are several fully equipped and furnished bungalow chalets, grassy picnic areas, and at the western end of the island a S$30million Marine Aquaculture Centre.

Sandwiched between St John's Island and Kusu Island, **Lazarus Island** is also linked at one end to Pulau Seringat. Recreational developments are planned by the Sentosa Leisure Group with plans to possibly turn Lazarus into a resort. The island has arguably the best beach in Singapore but not too many people know about it.

There is currently no infrastructure on Lazarus except for one beach pavilion, so there's nothing to do but swim, wander along the shore, jump on the internet or read a book.

You need to stock up on drinks and food before going as there are no shops on St. John's and Lazarus Island. There are no toilet or shower facilities at the beach. The nearest toilet facility is housed in a building next to the private jetty on Lazarus Island. There are toilets on St John's Island though. Camping is not allowed on St John's, Lazarus or Kusu islands.

**Kuso Island** is the most developed but it is still minimal. According to legend, a tortoise turned itself into an island to save two shipwrecked sailors – one Malay and one Chinese. This island is popular for its lagoons, pristine beaches, its wishing well and Tortoise Sanctuary. It also has two man-made attractions and excellent views of Singapore's mainland.

The **Da Bo Gong Temple** is a little Taoist temple built in 1923 by a wealthy businessman, with two main deities who are said to have the power to confer prosperity, cure diseases, calm the sea, avert danger, and give male children. This is the focal point of the yearly Kusu Festival (Oct-Nov), when pilgrims come to the island to pray for prosperity.

**Keramat Kusu** is an unusual Muslim shrine, painted bright yellow and dedicated to the saint Syed Abdul Rahman and his family, who lived here in the 19th century. It is located at the top of 152 steps and devotees pray for wealth, good marriage, good health and children.

Camping is allowed on **Pulau Hantu** with a permit. This can be obtained via email (administrator@sentosa.com.sg). You need to provide your name and contact number, camping dates, and the number of campers wishing to stay.

# 8 JURONG AND WEST SINGAPORE

Some years ago when Singapore was trying to expand and widen its tourism appeal, several attractions were developed in the industrial town of Jurong. They were a great success initially but then become over shadowed somewhat, but several have regained their appeal and are now justifiably popular with both locals and visitors.

The central north area contains the spectacular primary rainforests and mangrove swamps, some of which have been preserved in nature reserves and the Zoological Park. While they are spread out over a wider area than those in previous chapters, most are readily reachable by public transport.

We will start at the Pasir Panjang MRT station (CC26). The first place we visit is now a World War II interpretive centre.

**Reflections at Bukit Chandu** (Pasir Panjang Road) (http://www.yoursingapore.com/en_au/see-do-singapore/history/memorials/reflections-at-bukit-chandu.html), located at the peak of Opium Hill, is in a black and white Mock Tudor bungalow built more than 100 years ago by the colonial government for senior army officers.

During the Second World War, the house was being used to store military and food supplies. It was the site of one of the fiercest and last significant battles before the British surrendered Singapore to the Japanese in 1942.

The museum's exhibition gallery covers the history of World War II in Malaya, with exhibits, photographs, maps and artifacts. The Centre is connected to the Kent Ridge Park, a popular venue for bird watchers and eco-tourists, via a tree-top canopy walk.

To reach our next point of interest it is probably easier to return to the station and take a train one stop west to Haw Par Villa MRT. Unsurprisingly this is close to Haw Par Villa (262 Pasir Panjang Road), our next attraction.

**Haw Par Villa** (262 Pasir Panjang Road) (http://www.yoursingapore.com/see-do-singapore/culture-heritage/heritage-discovery/haw-par-villa.html) is a free "theme park" filled with strange life-sized statues of humanized animals, scary Chinese mythological characters, and plenty of gory dioramas. The main attraction - the *Ten Courts of Hell* depicts in gruesome detail what punishments befall sinners in hell. A visit here tells you much about traditional Chinese culture and it is quirky and fun.

There are more than 1,000 statues and dioramas glorifying Buddhist, Taoist and Confucian folklore. It was built in 1937 by brothers Aw Boon Haw and Aw Boon Par from profits made from the still-popular medicinal paste called Tiger Balm. It was once a place where parents would bring children for an education in morality but times are now changing. Later it became an amusement park with rides but this was not successful and many of the original statues have been returned.

A further one-stop on the MRT takes us to Kent Ridge station (CC24) and the **National University of Singapore** (21 Lower Kent Ridge Road) (www.nus.edu.sg/). This is the oldest and largest higher learning institute in Singapore. The NUS Museum, which opens every day except Monday and public holidays, focuses primarily but not exclusively on south-east Asian art and culture. It has over 7000 artifacts and artworks divided across four collections.

Also at the University is the new **Lee Kong Chian Natural History Museum** (LKCNHM) (http://lkcnhm.nus.edu.sg/) which has its origins in the Raffles Museum which was founded in 1849. The Zoological Reference Collection is internationally renowned and the NUS Herbarium documents the rich plant resources in south-east Asia. The highlight for many, however, will be the three Diplodocid Sauropod dinosaurs.

The main gallery consists of 15 zones, tracing the history of life on earth. Different sections are devoted to the origin of life and all major branches of the Tree of Life. This includes green plants, fungi, molluscs, arthropods, "fish", amphibians, "reptiles", birds, and mammals.

On the mezzanine floor is the heritage zone, where the history of the Raffles Museum and LKCNHM forms the backdrop to the history of natural history in Singapore. The cost of S$21 seems a bit high and you need to pre-book tickets for a specific time.

A visit is highly recommended for parents with young kids and you can spend up to 90 minutes here. The museum does not have a cafeteria on premises but there is a snack bar with hot and cold drinks at the museum gift shop.

If wandering around the campus or visiting the museums has little appeal, continue on the train to Buona Vista station (EW21/CC22) then change to the East-West line and go on to Jurong East MRT (EW24/NS1). It's a short walk from here to the Science Centre or catch Bus 66 or 335 at the Jurong East bus interchange and alight 2 stops later.

Jurong is now a major retail hub with several new shopping centers opened recently. These include. Westgate, Jem, IMM, JCube, and Big Box. If you are staying in Singapore for an extended visit or need some retail therapy in a compact environment then I would recommend visiting the area.

Westgate (http://westgate.com.sg/) has an Isetan department store, and the Isetan Food Hall, plus Fitness First, and many food outlets and technology shops. It also has good toddler entertainment facilities with a children's train to take the youngsters around the shops and there is a children's play area as well.

Jem (http://www.jem.sg/) has a large supermarket in the basement and the discount shop "Giant". There are also outlets for Robinsons, M&S, H&M, Topshop, Uni Qlo and many restaurants, IT outlets, fashion and beauty shops.

IMM (http://www.imm.sg/) is said to be the largest outlet shop in Singapore with many international brands having shops in the Centre. There is a free bus from Westgate, but it is close enough to walk and you then avoid the line for the free bus.

Big Box (http://www.bigbox.com.sg) is the newest addition to the area with a mix of homeware and discount supermarket.

JCube (http://www.jcube.com.sg/en/) has an ice skating rink and movie theatre.

The **Science Centre Singapore** (15 Science Centre Road) (www.science.edu.sg/) is acknowledged as one of the world's top science museums. It has twelve exhibition galleries with more than 1,000 interactive exhibits and is recommended for both adults and children. One of the highlights for me is the Human Body experience and I would definitely recommend paying the extra cost to do it as it is really neat climbing through a replica of the insides of a human body.

A five-minute walk along a covered walkway from Science Centre will get you to the Omni-Theatre and it is only meters from there to **Snow City** (www.snowcity.com.sg/), Singapore's only permanent indoor snow centre. This has a chamber with a 400 mm depth of snow and a 60 meter long slope which is about 3 storey's high.

You can slide down the snow slope while sitting on an inflatable tube and wine and dine on level 2, at Alpine Lodge. If you are from an area that gets regular snow, you are unlikely to be stunned but it is impressive that this can be built on the Equator.

Admission to the Science Centre is S$12 for adults and S$8 for children. The Omni Theatre is S$12 or S$14 depending on the movie for adults and children while Snow City is S$15 for everyone for a one-hour session. Two in One and Three in One packages are available and are excellent value.

The **Japanese Garden** (Yuan Ching Road) is built on an artificial island in the Jurong Lake area and is connected to the adjacent Chinese Garden by a beautiful bridge. The Japanese garden is designed to evoke inner peace and a meditative state during a visit. With its traditional arched bridges, 10 stone lanterns, traditional house and rest house, ponds and marble chip paths it faithfully recreates the traditional Japanese style. There is a small admission fee to the Turtle & Tortoise Museum.

The **Chinese Garden** (Chinese Garden Road off Yuan Ching Road) (http://www.yoursingapore.com/see-do-singapore/nature-wildlife/parks-gardens/chinese-garden.html ) is mostly built in the northern Chinese imperial style. There is a seven-storey pagoda, a replica of the stone boat at the Summer Palace in Beijing and a small southern-style garden with fine details, small rocks and 2000 pots of bonsai.

Rising from the cultivated gardens are features built to integrate and to be in harmony with the natural environment. It is visually stimulating but is also a great place to soak up the tranquility as you stroll along the meandering footpaths and take in the beauty of the woven plants, rocks and gentle stream.

After you have had your fill of tranquility, walk to the adjacent Chinese Garden MRT station (EW25) then go two stops to Boon Lay (EW27). Here you will find several other attractions. From the station take bus service No 251 or 194 to reach the Bird Park which is located near the base of Jurong Hill.

**Jurong Bird Park** (2 Jurong Hill) (www.birdpark.com.sg/) is arguably the world's best bird park. Enormous aviaries are filled with lush jungle plants and trees, as well as hundreds of different colored birds. The Waterfall Aviary (probably my favorite), Penguin Coast, World of Darkness, the *Kings of the Skies* show at the Hawk Arena, and the *High Flyers* show at the Pools Amphitheatre are all top attractions.

A big draw card for many is the Lory aviary where you walk around on walkways at tree level and are able to feed the birds, who fly down to you. There is a tram ride (S$5) that brings you to strategic stops all around the park and this is useful as the park is quite large. There is a nice cafe and shop inside the park. Adult admission is S$28, and children S$18. It opens 8.30 a.m.to 6 p.m.

You will be spending quite some time outdoors here so it is wise to bring sunglasses, sunblock, mosquito spray and an umbrella. Comfortable footwear and water are musts. You should be aware that the birds are on well-balanced diets and you are not being kind to them by feeding them.

The **Tiger Brewery Tour** (459 Jalan Ahmad Ibrahim) (https://www.tigerbrewerytour.com.sg/) is further to the west. From the Boon Lay MRT station you take bus service 182 from the interchange. If you've ever wondered how beer is made, this tour will certainly help explain things to you. You learn about the brewing process and the history of Tiger beer on the interactive 45-minute tour.

You can try your hand at pouring a draught beer in the packaging gallery and enjoy a 45-minute unlimited tasting of seven brews at the Tiger Tavern. All this costs adults S$18 and children S$12. There are tours at

10 and 11 a.m. and 1, 2, 4 and 5 p.m. Monday to Friday. You need a photo identity card for admission into the brewery.

Another unique attraction in this area is the Thow Kwang Pottery Jungle and Dragon Kiln (85 Lorong Tawas) (https://potteryjungle.wordpress.com/). You take bus 199 from the Boon Lay MRT station. Thow Kwang initially produced latex cups, and orchid pots from a huge dragon kiln, which is now the oldest brick built kiln in Singapore.

They now make ceramic dining wares, vases, indoor/outdoor pots, wooden furniture, ceramics stools, urns, lamps, famous Peranakan wares, figurines and other products. The kiln is of equal attractiveness. It is built on a gentle slope and is 27m long.

To reach the last attraction in this part of Singapore go two further stops on the MRT to Joo Koon station (EW29). The **Singapore Discovery Centre** (510 Upper Jurong Road) (www.sdc.com.sg/) is a 10 minute walk from here. It has been described as an art gallery, science museum and outdoor play area all in one but it is actually a military display. It opens Tuesday to Sunday from 9 a.m. to 6 p.m.

It strives to share the Singapore story through a wide range of multi-media interactive presentations and games with insights into the nation's challenges, dreams and aspirations but probably doesn't have a lot of appeal to visitors.

There are plenty of different packages starting at S$10 for adults and S$6 for children, which include admission to the centre, a bus tour of the Singapore Military Institute and a short 3D movie. There are some 4D simulation rides or you can battle at the outdoor paintball arena. For a calmer activity you can take the pedalos out on the large lake that fringes the centre. It is in the same neighborhood as the Army Museum so it is also possible to combine both attractions in a day.

The day will be gone for most people after covering all these places but I'll assume you are super-human and keep going. Take the MRT back to

Bukit Gombak station (NS3). From there you need to take bus 173 at the interchange.

**Bukit Timah Nature Reserve** (Hindhede Drive) is a small 164 hectare (400 acre) reserve near the geographic centre of Singapore Island. As you trek within Bukit Timah Nature Reserve, you can journey back in time to the days before Sir Stamford Raffles arrived, when much of the island was covered with lowland, tropical forest.

Nee Soon Swamp at the Central Catchment Nature Reserve is separated from the nature reserve by an expressway but a bridge allows wildlife to pass between the two reserves. According to the visitors' guide the two reserves are home to more than 840 flowering plants and over 500 species of animals.

Bukit Timah is excellent for strolling, running and hiking. Some people use the area to rock climb, abseil and go mountain biking. There are specially-allocated mountain-bike trails and a number of hiking trails including one that leads to Singapore's highest point (a staggering 163 meters above sea level!).

The Bukit Timah Nature Reserve was officially declared as an ASEAN Heritage Park in 2011. It is currently being upgraded and several areas are closed to the public but it is still worth a visit and will be even more attractive when it fully reopens late in 2016.

While the works are in progress, the nearby **MacRitchie Nature Trails** through the Central Catchment Reserve have even more appeal. There are boardwalks skirting the edge of the scenic MacRitchie Reservoir and walking trails through the forest. Several colored trails take from 1.5 to 3.5 hours to complete.

One 3 km walking and jogging track starts in the south-east of the reserve and finishes near the Singapore Island Country Club. Another popular attraction is the TreeTop Walk, a 250 m aerial bridge which reaches a height of 25 m above the ground. This is a 250-meter aerial free standing suspension bridge spanning the two highest points within

MacRitchie offering a bird's eye view of the plants and animals that live in the forest canopy.

The 11 km walking trail that circumnavigates the reservoir is an excellent way to take in the area's natural attractions. There are no maps available, but map boards situated along the trails and directional signage at junctions will help you find your way. You'll likely bump into long-tailed macaque monkeys, squirrels and monitor lizards. You need to have water and good shoes and if you bring snacks, have it in zipper bags (otherwise monkeys will smell it and hassle you).

You can rent kayaks at the Paddle Lodge for some fun in the water. There is a designated area for beginners, and another one for experienced paddlers.

East of here is the vast, modern **Kong Meng San Phor Kark See Temple** (88 Bright Hill Drive) (www.kmspks.org/), the largest Buddhist temple in Singapore, set in very attractive gardens. It is worth seeing but it is difficult to reach from here so I am giving it a miss. If you are keen to visit, take the MRT to Bishan station (CC15/NS17) then bus 40 from there.

Some way south of the temple is another attraction I have not covered elsewhere. The **Sun Yat Sen Nanyang Memorial Hall** (12 Tai Gin Road) (www.sysnmh.org.sg/) is where Dr Sun Yat Sen, the leader of China's nationalist movement, lived for some time. There are six exhibition halls in the 1900s Victorian-style bungalow which depict some 400 photographs and life-size wax figures amongst other items. A statue of Dr Sun is in front of the building. You can reach here on bus 21 from Novena MRT station (NS20).

Retuning to our original trail, the **Old Ford Motor Factory** (Upper Bukit Timah Road) (www.nas.gov.sg/moff/) is an historic building not far from Bukit Timah. It was built in 1941 to assemble cars then later it was used to assemble fighter planes. It is where the British surrendered to the Japanese in 1942, at the end of the Battle of Singapore.

The building now houses a World War II exhibition gallery called *Memories at Old Ford Factory*. It shows life in Singapore under Japanese rule using newspaper clips, maps and historical artefacts. A theatre screens documentaries showing different aspects of life during the occupation. Take the time to visit the garden plot behind the gallery which features wartime crops with explanations of the plant life.

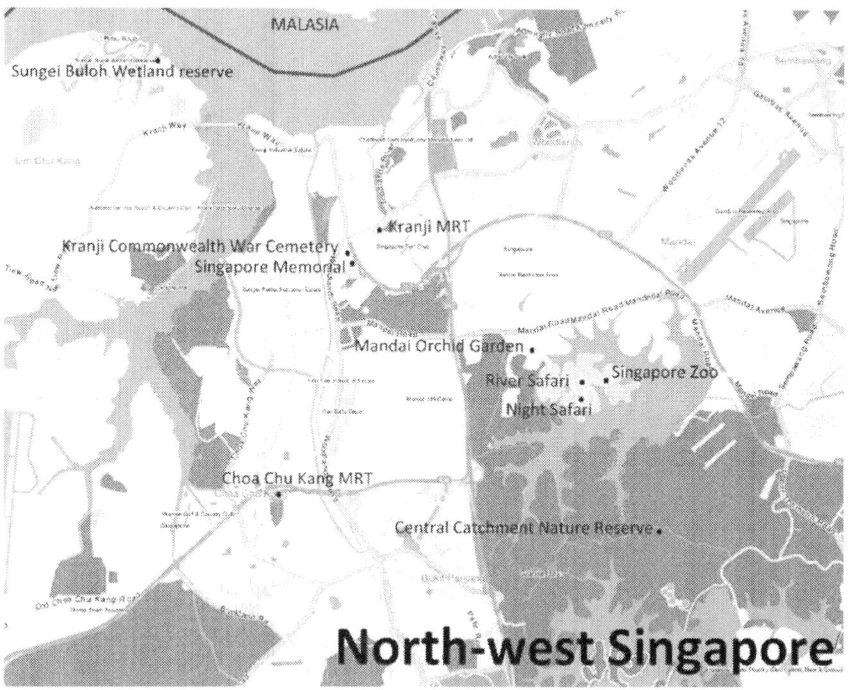


The next attraction is the Singapore Zoo and the most practical way to get there is by a short taxi ride. Taxis should be available along Upper Bukit Timah Road but there is always the fallback position of returning to the Bukit Gombak MTR station then going one more station to Choa Chu Kang (NS4). From here bus 927 goes to the zoo.

**Singapore Zoo** (80 Mandai Lake Road) (www.zoo.com.sg/) has one of the most beautiful wildlife park settings in the world as it is nestled within the lush Mandai rainforest. It contains more than 2,800 animals representing over 300 species of mammals, birds and reptiles. You can travel around the park onboard a guided tram or trek on foot at your own leisurely pace.

There are walk-through exhibits that bring animals and visitors together in one space for intimate encounters, underwater galleries to see the otters, pygmy hippos and giant estuarine crocodiles, and glass observatories to see cheetahs and lions. The *Great Rift Valley of Ethiopia* exhibit has around 90 baboons and other Ethiopian creatures in a very realistic setting.

A personal favorite of mine is the award-winning *Jungle Breakfast with Wildlife* program where you enjoy an international buffet in the company of several free-ranging orangutans. Families will probably enjoy the *Elephants at Work and Play Show* and the sea lions in the *Splash Safari Show*. There are elephant and camel rides. Admission is S$32 for adults, S$21 for children and S$14 for seniors. Opening hours are 8.30 a.m. to 6 p.m. daily.

**Night Safari** (80 Mandai Lake Road) (www.nightsafari.com.sg/) occupies 35 hectares (86 acres) of secondary rainforest adjacent to the Zoo. It houses over 2,500 animals representing over 130 species. Night Safari is an open-air zoo that is only open at night. It is divided into seven zones, which can be explored either on foot via four walking trails, or by tram.

I strongly suggest you do both. You are separated from the animals by natural barriers and the enclosures simulate the animals' native habitat in the Himalayan foothills, the jungles of Africa and various parts of south-east Asia.

Tribal dances, blowpipe demonstrations and fire eating displays are popular and most will enjoy the *Creatures of the Night Show* presented by the animals at 9.30 p.m. There are a few pre-planning activities which will make your visit more enjoyable. These include having an umbrella or raincoat handy in case of rain, wearing something that will give you maximum cover and is light in weight and color, wearing comfortable shoes and bringing insect repellent.

Adult admission is S$42 and children S$28. Opening times are 7.30 p.m. until mid-night with the restaurants & retail shop open from 5.30 p.m. daily. For those who want more you can explore in VIP style on the Safari Adventurer Tour. You are escorted for three hours by a personal tour guide who will share with you intimate insights about the park and its residents. The cost is S$140 for adults and S$95 for children. There is also a Premium Adventure Tour at higher cost.

The third attraction at this same site is **River Safari**

(www.riversafari.com.sg/), a river-themed zoo and aquarium which opened in 2013. The park consists of 10 different ecosystems around the world, including the Nile, Yangtze, Mississippi and Amazon rivers. It claims to have 5000 animals of 300 species and be the world's largest freshwater aquarium.

The *Amazon Flooded Forest* exhibit, which houses the manatees and various South American fish is said to be the largest freshwater aquarium in the world.

The park also has a pair of giant pandas which are housed in a specially constructed climate-controlled enclosure. The park features a short boat ride called the *Amazon River Quest* available at S$5 extra cost. All the attractions except the boat ride are under shelter so the weather has little impact on your visit. Food is available at the River Safari Tea House and Mama Panda Kitchen and there are some retail shops for souvenirs and collectables.

Because the attraction is still developing, I would recommend the main zoo if you have time and financial restrictions, but if pandas are your 'thing', this is the place. Admission is adults S$28 and children S$18. It opens from 9 a.m. to 6 p.m. daily. If you are really into animal parks a combined pass to the Zoo, Night Safari, River Safari and Jurong Bird Park is available for S$121 for adults and S$78 for children.

If you are staying in the central city and plan to visit any of the previous three attractions, one way of getting there is with the Safari Gate bus (https://www.safarigate.com/depart.php) which leaves from Suntec every hour or so during the day. During the 45 minute ride to the parks a video is shown to help you plan your visit. When you are ready to leave there are buses back to the city hourly during the day and half-hourly from 9.30 p.m. to 11 p.m.

A taxi is the best way to access the next attraction but if you are really into public transport return to Chao Chu Kang MRT station then go two more stations north to Kranji (NS7). From here it is walkable to the

**Kranji Commonwealth War Cemetery** (9 Woodlands Road) (http://www.cwgc.org/find-a-cemetery/cemetery/2004200/KRANJI%20WAR%20CEMETERY), the final resting place for Allied soldiers who perished in Singapore and other parts of south-east Asia during World War II.

The Kranji area was previously a military camp and after the fall of Singapore, the Japanese established a prisoner-of-war camp here. As with other cemeteries around the world, the grounds are immaculately maintained by the Commonwealth War Graves Commission.

The **Singapore Memorial**, or the Kranji War Memorial (http://www.cwgc.org/find-a-cemetery/cemetery/2053500/SINGAPORE%20MEMORIAL), stands beside the cemetery. The information booklet explains that the columns represent the army, the cover over the columns is shaped after of the wings of a plane, and the vertical tower resembles the sail of a submarine.

The Memorial's walls inscribe over 24,000 names of allied servicemen whose bodies were never found. It is a very sublime, moving location.

The Singapore Turf Club racecourse is adjacent to Kranji MRT Station. Horse racing is staged all year round on almost every Friday and Sunday. The jewel in the crown of the racing calendar is without any doubt the S$3 million Group 1 Singapore Airlines International Cup which is held in May as part of the Singapore International Racing Festival.

Races from Australia, Hong Kong, South Africa, Malaysia, UK, France, Macau, Korea and occasionally Japan, Dubai, New Zealand and USA are also shown live at the Turf Club. The Singapore Turf Club also runs a subsidiary equestrian riding centre.

Many farms in the Kranji Countryside are open to the public and welcome visitors! You can tour farms and buy farm-fresh local produce during opening hours. A market happens every quarter and is the only authentic farmers' market in Singapore.

You can take the Kranji Countryside Express bus (http://kranjicountryside.com/plan-your-visit/transport) from Kranji MRT station to the Sungei Buloh Wetland Reserve, Nyee Phoe (Gardenasia), D'Kranji Farm Resort, Bollywood Veggies where you can do a walking tour), Hay Dairies Goat Farm (milking only happens from 9:00am-10:30am), and the Jurong Frog Farm.

The bus runs daily, including public holidays. The bus fare is S$3/head/roundtrip. Retain your ticket to hop on and off if you are planning to visit several farms using the bus within a day.

The **Sungei Buloh Wetland Reserve** (https://www.nparks.gov.sg/sbwr) is a 10-minute bus ride away from Kranji MRT station on the Kranji Express. This area has an unusually high variety of bird species, which included migratory birds from as far as Siberia on their way to Australia. Paths and boardwalks wind through mangroves, coconut groves and marshes. Observation hides are available along the way where visitors can observe the flora and fauna.

There is a visitor centre, a cafe and souvenirs. Construction works are currently ongoing for Phase 2 of the Sungei Buloh Wetland Reserve Masterplan and these works have closed some areas such as the Kranji Nature Trail until late 2014.

To prepare for a visit to the wetland reserve, visitors are advised to wear shoes and socks, long pants and long-sleeved shirt in preferably light colors, and apply insect repellent on exposed skin and clothing before entering the wetland reserve.

**Admiralty Park** is also in this general area. The best access is from Woodlands MRT station which is two stops from Kranji. This is situated in hilly terrain with the Sungei Cina River running through it,. Encompassing a diverse mix of secondary forest, mangrove, riverine and open grassland habitats, and home to more than 100 species of flora and fauna, the park is a favorite of nature lovers. There is a buffet restaurant on site.

# 9 EAST SINGAPORE

The east and north-east parts of Singapore Island are dominated by the huge airport but there are several visitor attractions as well. Some are quite specific but others are general areas where there is an opportunity to see different cultures and local activities.

This area is not high on the list for short-term visitors but it provides different experiences for those looking for something apart from shopping and the 'head-line' attractions. We will start at the Paya Lebar MRT station (EW8/CC9).

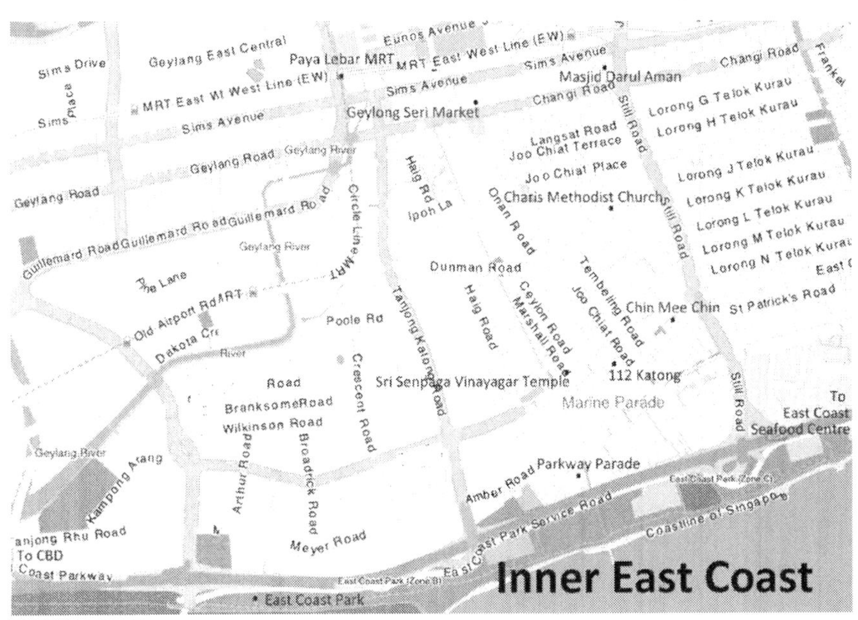

The first thing you notice is there are many Malay shops and restaurants in the area. Developments like Geylang Serai Market and festivities such as the Hari Raya Bazaars along Geylang Road contribute to the distinctive local Malay identity of the area. In fact the best time to visit here is during the Ramadan fasting month when the streets are ablaze with blinking lights and there are colourful street stalls. On leaving the station we cross Sims Avenue to Geylang Road.

**Geylang Serai Market** (1 Geylang Serai) has been a focal point for the local Malay community for 50 years. For 42 years, stallholders struggled with makeshift stalls in ramshackle conditions but in 2006, the aging market was torn down as part of a government redevelopment project. In 2010 a two-storey concrete block building with its distinctive three-tiered grand entryway was opened.

Now, the airy food centre sits on the second floor, while a wet market and a battery of shops laden with clothing, groceries, household goods and other bric-a-brac is on the ground floor. One of the most popular stalls here is Sinar Pagi Nasi Padang (Stall 137) which has a huge collection of dishes prepared in the Kapau Indonesian style. Many stalls have long queues in the busy periods and the wet market can get very crowded on weekends.

We exit the market to Changi Road and walk east to the **Masjid Darul Aman** (1 Jalan Eunos). This mosque is an excellent example of tropical architecture, with a pitched-roof commonly found in the Malay Archipelago. Built in 1986 and added to in 2005, the mosque can accommodate up to 3,500 people.

It’s now a question of going south through Joo Chiat to Katong. Both areas are home to many Eurasians and Peranakans. The Peranakans are descendants of 17$^{th}$ century Chinese and Indian immigrants who married non-Muslim natives from the Malay Archipelago. Joo Chiat is Singapore's first Heritage Town chosen, in part, because of its strong efforts to promote its Peranakan culture.

It was named after a wealthy Chinese landowner, Chew Joo Chiat, and the area is dotted with colourful shophouses and homes that are adorned by sculpted facades of animal reliefs and hand-crafted ceramic tiles. It has a reputation too, for the sleazy Vietnamese pubs and massage parlors along the main thoroughfare but these are slowly being replaced by new businesses such as art galleries, design studios, up-market retail outlets, boutique hotels and eateries.

Joo Chiat is dotted with small restaurants so after you get tired walking just go inside, order something to drink or eat and rest. You can download free walking tour booklets on the neighborhood from the Singapore Parks website.

The serene **Masjid Khalid** (Khalid Mosque) at 130 Joo Chiat Road is amidst the undulating rows of shophouses. Built in 1917 and recently renovated in 1998, the mosque was originally intended as a place of worship for Indian Muslims, and is today one of the gathering points of Katong/Joo Chiat's Malay community.

**The Intan** (69 Joo Chiat Terrace) (http://the-intan.com/2012/) will appeal to many visitors because it is different to most other attractions in Singapore. At this intimate museum you find an amazing collection of Peranakan furniture and decorative items, curated by Mr. Alvin Yapp. Note that visits are strictly by appointments only.

This is an enlightening walk through the history of Peranakan culture told through the very senses of a true blue *baba*. The host and The Intan itself is a treasure trove of all things Peranakan.

Also along here is the **Kuan Im Tng Temple** at 62 Tembeling Road This Chinese temple was built in 1921. Its ornate façade and front doors are flanked by circular windows, surrounded by yellow, white and blue mosaic symbols of the Eight Immortals. The green roof tiles are Chinese-made and its roof ridges are adorned with statues of dancing dragons. The main prayer hall is dedicated to the Goddess of Mercy, Confucius and the Sun and Moon Gods.

Further east on Joo Chiat Place is an architectural masterpiece. The **Lotus at Joo Chiat** apartments are a fine example of integrating old shophouses with new flats, and were built in the 1930s in the Late Shophouse style. This development received the Urban Redevelopment Authority's Architectural Heritage Award in 2002 for their excellent restoration.

Koon Seng Road is one of the best areas to see the lovely Baroque-style terrace houses in shades of peach, pale blue, green, orange, pink and lavender. They are outstanding examples of Singapore's architectural heritage. The designs are exceptionally ornate and the details exquisite, showcasing a fusion of Eastern and Western influences.

This is also where you will find the **Charis Methodist Church** (91 Koon Seng Rd). This grew from the English congregation of the Geylang Chinese Methodist Church and was constituted as a church in 1989. Presently there are two English services and one Mandarin service a week.

You can drop into the **Joo Chiat Community Club**, 405 Joo Chiat Road. It started as a humble wooden hut with simple facilities like a library, boys' club and basketball court, but the Joo Chiat Community Club has since been extensively renovated. Today it remains a meeting point for the community.

When we arrive at East Coast Road, our attention is immediately drawn to **112 Katong** (www.112katong.com.sg/about/the-mall/), a modern shopping complex at the intersection of East Coast Road and Joo Chiat Road. There are over 140 specialty shops and food outlets over six levels here so you may like to spend some time just wandering around.

Once filled with coconut plantations and used as a weekend retreat by wealthy city dwellers, **Katong** developed into a residential suburb by the early 20th century. The plantations have since gone, but you can still admire this vibrant neighborhood's many well-preserved Peranakan shophouses and a scattering of colonial bungalows.

The rebuilding of the nation after World War II and the independence of Singapore transformed the face of Katong/Joo Chiat. To retain its rich architecture and heritage, over 700 buildings in the area have been conserved. Today a trip to Katong is first and foremost a food trail that will take you through traditional *kopitiams* (coffee shops), Peranakan dining institutions, and multi-ethnic eateries.

A little further to the east is **Chin Mee Chin** (204 East Coast Road), one of the few old-school coffee shops left in Katong. It has a wonderful old world charm with its ceiling fans, marble-top tables and wooden chairs. Its simple breakfast of *kaya* toast, soft boiled eggs and coffee are its most famous items but I cannot resist the Custard Egg Tart and Custard Puffs. The outlet roasts its own coffee beans and bakes its own bread.

In fact in several areas you can explore cool cafes that sit next to old-world coffee shops selling the famous Katong 'laksa', 'kueh chang' (dumplings) and other Nonya delicacies. The 'laksa' (noodles in a spicy coconut-based broth) is supposed to be particularly good at 328 Katong Laksa (53 East Coast Road) – its heady flavors pack a punch.

Almost next door to Chin Mee Chin is **Katong Antique House** (208 East Coast Road) a fully restored bona fide Peranakan family home, and admire the many antiques and heirlooms worthy of any museum collection. Since inheriting the once-bare house in the 1970s, the owner has filled it with traditional Peranakan furniture and other antiques and heirlooms.

The top floor houses a small gallery, where you can admire intricately woven 'kasut manek' or beaded slippers, as well as wedding costumes.

Back to the west, there are several places to see. The Church of the Holy Family was a focal point for the Eurasian community of Katong/Joo Chiat. Its origins date from 1902, with the original chapel built in 1923. Today, it continues to serve the spiritual needs of the local Catholic community. The building was re-built in 1999, while the front sculptures have been retained from the original church structure.

Next is the conserved terrace houses at 150 East Coast Road These single-storey terrace houses stand beside a former sea wall near where the beach used to be. What makes these homes unusual is that the living area is built on raised ground to protect against the rising tides then. The architectural style is an eclectic mix of traditional local architecture infused with Western influences.

After crossing Joo Chiat Road you will see the former Tay Buan Guan Shop, at 113 East Coast Road. The Tay Buan Guan department store grew from this humble shophouse to a multi-storey shopping centre located to the rear of East Coast Road, and was one of Singapore's best-loved shopping hubs. This shophouse is now known as Rumah Bebe (Bebe's House), a Peranakan arts and crafts store-cum-museum.

At 75 East Coast Road stands the former Katong Bakery & Confectionery, also affectionately known as the "Red House" Bakery, once famous for its Swiss rolls and curry puffs. It was originally built as a private residence facing the sea and operated as a bakery for over 80 years until its closure in 2003. Fortunately the building has been preserved.

The **Sri Senpaga Vinayagar Temple** (19 Ceylon Road) is worth a visit. Built in the mid-19$^{th}$ century, it was rebuilt and consecrated in 2003. Two three meter tall demigod gatekeepers flank the entrance tower, which features the Chola style of architecture. Remove your shoes and socks before stepping inside to see the colourful murals depicting the stories of Lord Vinayagar, as well as four granite pillars featuring sculptures of 32 different forms of Lord Vinayagar.

The **St Hilda's** Anglican Church, built in 1934, is sandwiched between Ceylon and Fowlie Roads. Designed after a simple English parish church style, it features a conical tower built in the Victorian tradition. Look out for the beautiful stained glass in the chapel.

Now follow Brooke Road south to **Parkway Parade** (80 Marine Parade) (www.parkwayparade.com.sg/) which has a 17-floor office tower and a seven-storey shopping mall with a basement. It was one of Singapore's first major and biggest suburban malls and is a major centre for this area and is a good place to grab a quick lunch. There are over 250 stores including Best Denki, Giant Hypermarket, Isetan and Food Republic.

Across the road is the 10 km long **East Coast Park** (https://www.nparks.gov.sg/gardens-parks-and-nature/parks-and-nature-reserves/east-coast-park) which stretches from Marina Bay to Changi Airport. This is the largest park in Singapore and is a highly popular hangout for couples, groups of friends and families. The shoreline has palm trees, shady area and places to sit while the more active can walk, jog or cycle on well-defined paths.

If you are seeking some sporting action this park has facilities for beach volleyball, cycling, cable skiing and various water sports. There is also an Xtreme SkatePark.

East Coast Park has an area of 185 hectares, and a 15 km scenic coastline. It attracts more than seven million visitors a year. It was opened in the 1970s, when the government completed land reclamation in the area.

You may like to take a taxi from here to the **East Coast Seafood Centre** (1206 E Coast Parkway), our next stop, although it is a pleasant walk through the park. This is best known for co-locating several major local seafood restaurants. Some signature local dishes are served here including the very popular chili crab and the black pepper crab. Don't wear your best clothes as things can get messy. Some of the restaurants offer sea view dining.

If you don't like seafood, just walk a few hundred meters further east around the lagoon and you will find the **East Coast Lagoon Food Village**. This is down-market from the Seafood Centre and while there is still seafood on the menu this hawker centre has many other options.

The location here is unique and you can walk barefoot off the beach and order up some satay, pig's trotters, BBQ chicken or other dishes with a beer, and not feel out of place. At night with the breeze coming off the water and the lights from the hundreds of cargo ships anchored offshore glistening in the water, it would be hard to find a more attractive place. There are several satay stalls, and places selling Oyster omelet, Wanton Mee, BBQ Chicken Wings, duck rice, and many other favorites.

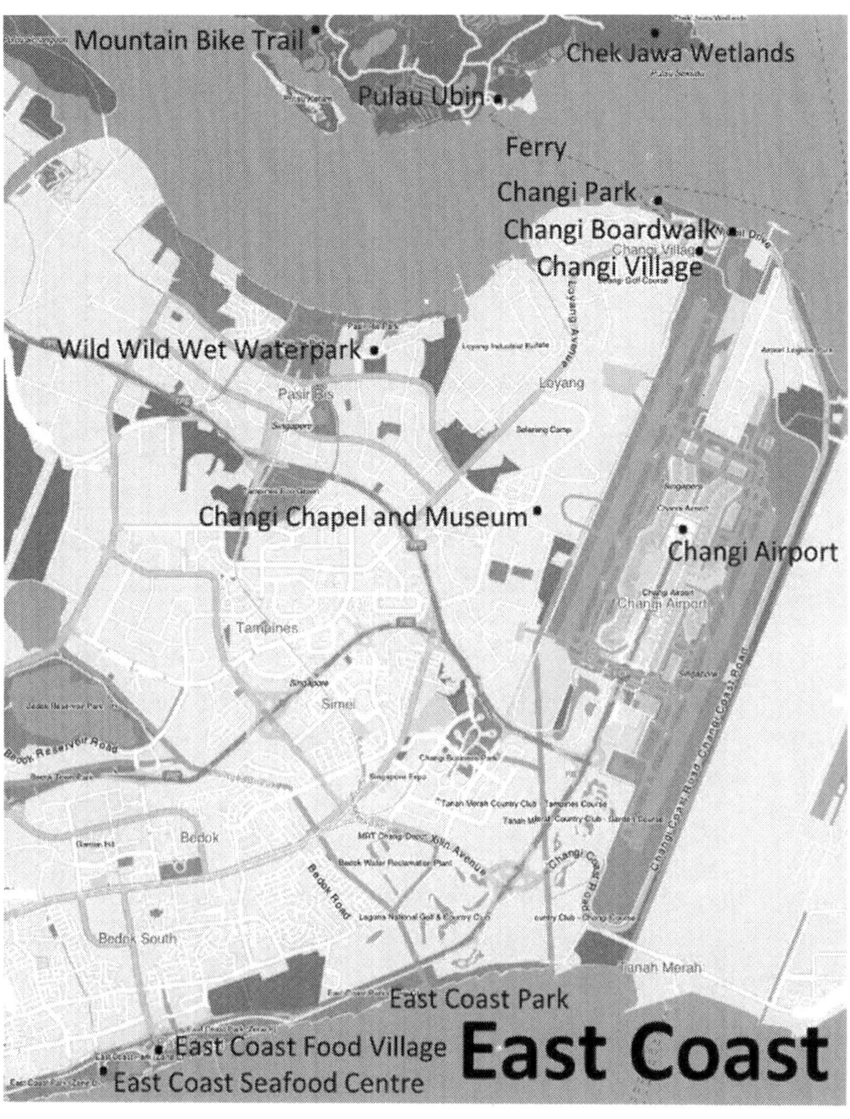

Singapore has two major limitations -- land and clean water. To find out more about water you can visit the **NEWater Visitor Centre** (http://www.pub.gov.sg/water/newater/visitors/Pages/default.aspx) at 20 Koh Sek Lim Road. Tours are free but must be booked online or via telephone at 65467874

The tour shows how Singapore is tackling the problem of having enough clean water for a growing population. The water treatment scheme of Singapore is amazing and a visit lets you learn about it, through an interactive way, in a very professional guided tour.

Another place that will appeal to some visitors is the **Republic of Singapore Navy Museum** (112 Tanah Merah Coast Road) on the eastern side of Changi Airport. This is a place you probably need to visit by taxi as it is quite isolated from the other attractions. The museum has numerous interior displays and there are old guns and weapon systems from decommissioned ships in an outdoor exhibit.

The young and the young at heart can try their hands at taking out simulated enemy targets with the weapons that the Navy possesses, navigate a ship through the busy Singapore Strait, steer a submarine underwater, or get a glimpse of what it is like to be a commanding officer of a frigate. Admission is free but it is not open on Sundays or public holidays.

You need to take a taxi from here to the **Changi Chapel and Museum** (1000 Upper Changi Rd North) (http://www.changimuseum.sg/). This is dedicated to Singapore's history during the Japanese occupation in World War II and specifically the lives and experiences of the thousands of civilian and Allied prisoners of war who were held and mistreated in the Changi prison camp area.

As Changi Prison is still in use, Singapore built a replica Chapel and Museum next to it in 1988 so the public could get access to some of the reminders of this horrendous period. When Changi Prison was expanded in 2001, the Chapel and Museum was relocated to its present site one kilometer away.

The Museum has a collection of paintings, photographs and personal effects donated by former POWs and a series of magnificent wall paintings called The Changi Murals, painstakingly recreated from the originals painted by Bombardier Stanley Warren. The murals played an important role during the Second World War, as they gave hope to the Allied POWs, including Stanley Warren himself, through prayers and worships.

Visitors are also able to view screenings of two videos. There is a research area that houses a collection of rare books and literature depicting life during the war years.

The Changi Chapel allows visitors to light a candle to remember those who were held at Changi during the war. There are Sunday services conducted by various church groups every Sunday. Visitors are welcome to join these services. There is no admission charge to the museum but the excellent audio-guide costs adult/child S$8/4 for those who really want to understand this place of suffering, resilience and hope.

**Changi Village** is a modern village at the northern end of Changi Airport with a smart, modern hotel, a bus terminal, and a ferry terminal with small passenger ferries heading to Pulau Ubin and also to some destinations in Johor, Malaysia. With its rich history, lush coastal greenery and many gastronomical delights, Changi Village is certainly a unique Singaporean neighborhood which is worth visiting.

One of the popular attractions here is the hawker centre. This has a popular nasi lemak stall, where long queues are often seen, and other stalls selling delicious wanton and other dishes. Several monkeys are in the area so do not leave your belongings or food unprotected. Many residents living in nearby estates drive to Changi Village for drinks in the evening so many of the coffee shops are open past midnight. There are cafés, pubs, and Western and Chinese restaurants to suit all budgets.

Apart from the infamous prison, Changi has been associated with other tragedies. Changi Beach was the location of a mass execution of Chinese who were rounded up by the Japanese soldiers during World War II but there is no reminder of that today. Now you need to be aware of the transvestites who loiter near the car park of the Changi Point ferry terminal waiting for customers.

More than 50,000 Allied prisoners-of-war were marched to Changi by the Japanese in World War II. Batches were then sent to the borders of Thailand and Burma for the construction of the infamous Burma Railway, also known as the "Death Railway" as many of them did not survive to return.

The **Sree Ramar Temple** (51 Changi Village Road) is a fairly simple affair with a statue of Hindu deity Lord Rama flanked by smaller figurines, on a platform. The entire structure is a light shade of pink, a color that also coats the temple's walls, It is interesting that Buddhists and Taoists also visit the temple to pay their respects to the statues of Buddha and the Goddess of Mercy that are set up within the temple's compounds.

A good attraction is the 2 km long **Changi Boardwalk**, located on the western part of Changi Point. It connects the Changi Beach Club, the Changi Sailing Club and the Changi Point Ferry. The best time to visit is in the late afternoon to catch the sunset.

**Changi Beach Park** is one of the oldest coastal parks in Singapore and it brings back memories for those who visited in the sixties and seventies. The 3.3 km long linear park has some nice white beaches dotted with coconut palms, and there are BBQ pits, park benches and shelters for visitors. You can also experience seafront dining here at Bistro @ Changi. There is a skate and bicycle kiosk, toilets with outdoor shower facilities and an Adventure Playground.

The Changi Sailing Club (http://www.csc.org.sg/) (32 Netheravon Rd.) is a nice place to visit here. Non members can use the dining room which is on the first floor with open sides providing lovely views over the beach and sea. The menu offers Western and Asian food. Food quality is good and the prices are fine for what is a lovely location with good service.

It may not be a place for everyone but **Pulau Ubin** (http://www.wildsingapore.com/ubin/), the last 'kampung' (village) in Singapore, is great for those who want a peek into life in Singapore in the 1960s. You reach here by bumboat from Changi and bicycles, which can be rented from the island jetty, are best for exploring the island. When you arrive at Pulau Ubin, go for a nature walk called the Sensory Trail next to the jetty before renting a bicycle.

As you peddle along rustic roads under swaying coconut palms, you can explore shady trails in overgrown rubber plantations, and check out secluded beaches and flourishing mangroves. Admission to the island is free, but regular boat services only run during daylight hours.

The small village where you land is a collection of old wooden buildings with bicycle rental shops, restaurants and the odd provision shop. There are quite a few lunch options in Ubin Town, including affordable seafood eateries.

**Chek Jawa Wetlands** (https://www.nparks.gov.sg/gardens-parks-and-nature/parks-and-nature-reserves/pulau-ubin-and-chek-jawa) is a popular destination for visitors as there are great bird and marine life spotting opportunities. You can ride here or walk in about 40 minutes along a track lined with rubber trees.

Chek Jawa Wetlands has an information kiosk which is open 8.30 a.m. to 5 p.m., boardwalk, viewing tower, and viewing jetty. The information centre, built in Tudor style, is probably the only building in Singapore with a working fireplace.

If you plan to visit, there are a few things to keep in mind. Ubin operates on cash so bring money with you. Put on some insect repellent to keep the mosquitoes at bay and don't provoke the wild boar and monkeys which exist all over the island.

For those fitness enthusiasts there is a superb mountain bike trail network and the 45 hectare Ketam Mountain Bike Park, an all-weather, manmade route that has solidified the island's unofficial title of "Bicycle Island".

Back on the main island, **Wild Wild Wet Waterpark** (1 Pasir Ris Close) (www.wildwildwet.com/) is Singapore's largest water theme park and the final attraction for us. The park opens Monday and Wed to Fri 1 p.m. to 7 p.m. and weekends and public holidays 10 a.m. to 7 p.m. This is part **Downtown East**, which is a major lifestyle, recreational and entertainment hub catering to the wide interests of youths and families by bringing exciting activities and fun facilities all under one roof.

Downtown East is home to Costa Sands Resort, and there is also the entertainment and leisure centre E!hub, featuring a cinema, an arcade, Orchid Bowl and eXplorerkid, one of Singapore's largest indoor family playground.

Nearby **Pasir Ris Park** offers another pleasant stretch of beach with some casual eateries. There is also a mangrove swamp with a boardwalk across the mudflats providing viewing opportunities of migratory birds and other fauna and flora..

# 10 A SHORT HISTORY

I would like to thank the Singapore Government and several other sources for the information in this chapter.

It is believed that the first residents of Singapore migrated to the area between 2500 and 1500 B.C. Early contact with seafaring traders from India caused them to incorporate Hinduism with the local animist beliefs. The first written record was in the third century A.D. when a Chinese account describes an island which it called Pu Luo Chung. By the seventh century Singapore had become a trading port for many nationalities.

The Indian Chola Empire invaded Singapore in the 11$^{th}$ century but little is known of this period. Few records exist even for future years but there is a reference in a 17$^{th}$-century Malay document stating that in 1299 the city of Singapura ("lion city") was founded after a strange, lion-like beast that had been sighted there.

In 1320, a trade mission from the Mongol Empire came to what is believed to be Singapore. A Chinese traveler, visited the island a few years later, and described a small settlement with both Malay and Chinese residents. A Javanese poem written some 40 years later also referred to a settlement on the island called Temasek. Recent finds at Fort Canning indicate that Singapore was a port way back in the 14$^{th}$ century.

During this period, Siam and the Java-based Majapahit Empire both wanted control of the Malay Peninsula and the Singapore ruler Iskandar

Shah was forced to Malacca by a Majapahit attack. He then founded the Sultanate of Malacca and became a powerful ruler who used Singapore as a trading port. The town was influenced when the Hindu ruler of Malacca, converted to Islam.

In the early 15$^{th}$ century, Singapore was paying tribute to Siam, but the Malacca Sultanate soon gained authority over the island. Singapore remained loyal to the Sultanate even after the Portuguese seizure of Malacca in 1511.

In 1613, the Portuguese burned down the trading post and after that, the island was largely abandoned. It was nearly 200 years before agriculture activities returned to Temasek and in 1818 it was settled by a Malay official of the Johore Sultanate.

The British now enter the picture. In 1818, Stamford Raffles was sent to the British colony at Bencoolen on the west coast of Sumatra. Raffles hoped to establish a new port and then challenge the Dutch, who controlled the spice trade. He convinced the British East India Company, to let him seek a new British base in the region.

One year later he did a deal with the local Malay official to establish a trading post on the island he called Singapore. He opened the port to free trade and Singapore has hardly looked back since.

Raffles then returned to Bencoolen but returned to Singapore in 1822 to draft a set of policies for the settlement and to better organized the town. The following year he departed for Britain and would never return.

Singapore grew in size and prosperity and by 1827 Chinese had become the main ethnic group. From 1826 to 1867, Singapore and several other places were ruled together as the Straits Settlements from the Indian headquarters of the British East India Company.

During this period, the administration struggled to cope. By 1850 the population had grown to nearly 60,000 people and prostitution, gambling, and drug abuse was widespread. Gang wars were common between Chinese criminal secret societies.

In 1867 the British acted by making the Straits Settlements a crown colony ruled directly from London. A governor was installed and executive and legislative councils created. By that time, Singapore was the most important part of the Straits Settlements as it had grown to become a bustling seaport with 86,000 inhabitants.

The opening of the Suez Canal brought still greater maritime activity to Singapore. Later in the century and into the twentieth century, Singapore became a major port for Malaya.

The city continued to grow and there was some unrest about colonial rule but this became unimportant in 1942 when the Japanese invaded. Singapore was renamed Syonan-to and was occupied by the Japanese from 1942 to 1945. Harsh measures were imposed on the local population, with the Chinese population being particularly targeted.

By the time the Japanese surrendered in August 1945 much of the city's infrastructure had been destroyed and there was a shortage of food. To help the situation, in April 1946, Singapore became a separate Crown Colony with a civil administration headed by a Governor, but this failed to stop discontent.

There were political changes taking place and in 1947, separate Executive and Legislative Councils were established with six members of the Legislative Council to be elected. Three of the elected seats were won by the newly formed conservative Singapore Progressive Party (SPP). In 1951, when the number of elected seats increased to nine, the SPP won six seats.

Further changes occurred in 1955 when a new Legislative Assembly replaced the Legislative Council. A Chief Minister and a Council of Ministers were picked under a parliamentary system. The SPP was soundly defeated in the election, winning only four seats out of twenty-five, while the left-leaning Labour Front won ten seats and formed a coalition government with the UMNO-MCA Alliance. David Marshall, leader of the Labour Front, became the first Chief Minister of Singapore.

In 1956, Marshall pushed London for complete self-rule but when this failed he resigned. The new Chief Minister, Lim Yew Hock, took a hard line on communist and leftist groups which pleased the British Government and in 1957, complete internal self-government was agreed on.

Elections were held in 1959 and the People's Action Party (PAP) won in a landslide, taking forty-three of the fifty-one seats. Its leader Lee Kuan Yew, a young British-educated lawyer, became the first Prime Minister of Singapore.

The PAP government immediately encouraged economic development, revamped the education system and promoted the English language over the Chinese language.

Somewhat surprisingly, the PAP leaders believed that Singapore's future lay with Malaya and they campaigned vigorously for a merger. In 1961, Malaya's Prime Minister suggested a Federation of Malaysia, comprising the Federation of Malaya, Singapore, Brunei and the British territories of North Borneo and Sarawak.

Brunei refused to join but in September 1963, Malaya, Singapore, North Borneo and Sarawak were merged to form Malaysia. The union had immediate problems, however, with the Singapore Chinese feeling discriminated against by policies, which granted special privileges to the Malays.

At the same time Indonesian President Sukarno initiated military and other actions against the new nation. Indonesia also encouraged strife between the Malays and the Chinese.

In 1965 the Malaysian Prime Minister expelled Singapore from the Malaysian federation. The Singapore Parliament immediately establishing the island as an independent and sovereign republic. Yusof bin Ishak was appointed as its first President.

Singapore joined the United Nations in September 1965 and joined the Commonwealth in October. It co-founded the Association of Southeast Asian Nations (ASEAN) in 1967 and was admitted into the Non-Aligned Movement in 1970.

The government established industrial estates in the 1970s, and gave foreign investors tax incentives. Singapore also encouraged big oil companies to establish oil refineries in Singapore and the country soon became the third largest oil-refining centre in the world.

It was realized that the country needed better infrastructure so Changi Airport was opened in 1981 and Singapore Airlines was developed into a major airline while the Port of Singapore became one of the world's busiest ports. In 1987, the first Mass Rapid Transit (MRT) line began operation and by then Singapore had become an important transportation hub and a major tourist destination.

The political situation continued to be dominated by the People's Action Party. It won every parliamentary seat in every election between 1966 and 1981. The government, however, underwent several significant changes.

In 1984 up to three losing candidates from opposition parties were appointed as MPs. In 1988 multi-seat electoral divisions were created to ensure minority representation in parliament. In 1990 non-elected non-partisan MPs were allowed and in 1991 the Constitution was amended to provide for an Elected President.

Lee Kuan Yew retired in 1990 after more than 25 years and Goh Chok Tong, became the second prime minister. In 2004, Lee Hsien Loong, the eldest son of Lee Kuan Yew, became the third prime minister of Singapore and he remains so today. The PAP won 82 of the 84 parliamentary seats in 2006. In 2011 it won all but six seats, but opposition parties made unprecedented gains. Tony Tan was elected president.

Lee Kuan Yew died in 2015. In the 2015 election, out of 89 seats, PAP contested all and won 83, with the other 6 seats won by The Workers' Party of Singapore out of the 28 seats it contested. PAP achieved its best results since 2001 with 69.86% of the popular vote.

Issues such as the rising cost of living, immigration and income inequality are major challenges facing the government. The terrorism threat is certainly something that is heightened in Singapore and has become more prominent over the last two years with ISIS.

A major indication of Singapore's rising importance in Asian and world business was the 2015 announcement that the World Bank is expanding its Singapore office to create its first Infrastructure and Urban Development Hub.

In an official announcement the World Bank said the choice of Singapore for the hub that focuses on infrastructure and urban development is based on three factors: Singapore's unique role as a regional business and trade center, its strong position in world capital markets, and its remarkable development history.

# 11 ESSENTIALS

## Passports, Visas and Customs

All visitors must have a passport valid for at least six months from your date of entry. In theory you also require an onward or return ticket, entry facilities to the next destination, and sufficient funds to stay in Singapore although most visitors are not asked about these requirements. Visitors from a number of Middle Eastern, eastern European, African and selected Asian countries also require a visa. Further details are available from ica_feedback@ica.gov.sg/

If you are arriving from anywhere other than Malaysia, a visitor is allowed a small duty-free alcohol allowance. There are no concessions on cigarettes or other tobacco products. There are no restrictions on the amount of currency you can bring in. Prohibited items are similar to most countries except printed or recorded pornography is prohibited and pirated movies, music and software are also prohibited.

All visitors should be aware of Singapore's strict drug policy which prohibits importing, selling or using illegal narcotics. Punishments for those who violate this are severe and can include the death penalty. Don't be crazy and try your luck with the authorities.

## When to Go

The peak season in Singapore is from mid-December until after Chinese New Year (late January or early February). At this time most airlines and hotels are full. Hotel occupancy rates are high year-round in Singapore so there is little chance of negotiating a special price. This means that the weather and festivals can determine when you should go.

While there is some variation in temperature, Singapore is hot the whole year. Average monthly maximum temperatures vary between 30°C and 32°C with the highest being March to June and the lowest being December and January. Average monthly minimum temperatures are 24°C in November to February and 26°C in May and June. Rainfall is highest in November, December and January and lowest in February.

Some visitors will plan a visit to coincide with one of the various festivals which are held throughout the year. Some dates are given in a following section.

**Language**

Singapore has four official languages – Malay, Chinese Mandarin, Tamil and English. Most Singaporeans are therefore bilingual, if not multi-lingual. English is the first language taught in school and the main language used in the workplace. The predominant usage of English means visitors find it is one of the easiest countries in Asia to travel in and enjoy.

**Health and Safety**

Standards of health and hygiene are high in Singapore and there are world-class medical facilities. Some visitors experience stomach upsets from a change in diet and climate but this is generally not caused by unhygienic food or water. No inoculations or tablets are needed except if you have been to an area where yellow fever is prevalent. Tap water is safe to drink.

The tropical heat can be a problem to some people as it can cause dehydration and sunburn. The solution is to drink plenty of water, stay in the shade as much as possible, and protect yourself with a hat, sunscreen and sunglasses.

Pharmacies have all the common medications but it can be useful to have your own medical kit. Various medications cannot be bought in Singapore without a local doctor's prescription so you should bring some prescription medicines from home. Make sure these are properly labeled.

Singapore is one of the strictest countries in the world when it comes to penalties for possessing or smuggling narcotics. It should not be necessary to advise you that it is extremely foolish to have anything to do with drugs before or while in the country.

Crime rates in the city are low and police are quite vigilant but common sense safety rules apply here as anywhere else. It is wise to avoid carrying large sums of money or wearing expensive jewelry and you should keep your passport beneath clothing. There are certain areas where walking along dimly-lit streets late at night should be avoided.

## Currency and banking

Banking and money changing facilities are good. Banks open from 9.30 a.m. to 3 p.m. Monday to Friday and from 9.30 a.m. to 11.30.a.m. on Saturday. Cash and traveler's checks can be exchanged at large branches of all banks. Up-market hotels and some shopping centers will also exchange common world currencies. Licensed money changers operate for extended hours and sometimes offer the best rates.

ATM machines are extremely common but only issue the local currency. There is usually a daily withdrawal limit and a small fee is charged for the transaction. Visa and Mastercard credit cards are widely accepted and other cards less so. They can also be used at ATMs and banks.

The local currency is the Singapore dollar (S$) which is made up of 100 cents. Coins are issued in denominations of 5, 10, 20, 50 cents and one dollar. There are still some 1 cent coins in circulation but these have not been minted since 2003. Dollar notes are in denominations of 1, 2, 5, 10, 20, 50, 100, 500, and 1000 dollars.

The S1 note and S$10,000 note are slowly being phased out but are still legal currency. Notes have been produced both on paper and on polymer and you are likely to see both.

## Public Holidays and Festivals

The following are the official public holidays in 2016.

New Years Day - 1 January

Chinese New Year – 8-9 February

Good Friday – 25 March

Labour Day - 1 May

Vesak Day – 21 May

Hari Raya Puasa - 6 July

National Day - 9 August

Hari Raya Haji - 12 September

Deepavali – 29 October

Christmas Day - 25 December

Major festivals and events include Chinese New Year, Hindu festival of Thaipusam (January/February), Chinese Festival of the Arts (February), the Great Singapore Sale (June/July), Singapore Food Festival (July), Dragon Boat Festival (July), National Day celebrations (August), International Festival of the Arts (August/September), Singapore Grand Prix (September), Deepavali (October/November), and Singapore

International Film Festival (December).

## The Arts in Singapore

Singapore has not been particularly noted for its art scene until recently. That is rapidly changing with new international-style venues and a growing number of professional organizations.

The Singapore Dance Theatre presents both modern dance interpretations and classical performances. It performs at the Victoria Theatre, the University Cultural Centre and the Esplanade Theatre and also presents its *Ballet Under the Stars* on the Fort Canning lawn.

The Singapore Symphony Orchestra plays all the mainstream standard works as well as works by Asian composers. It is a full-time professional orchestra with 96 members, which performs at its home at the Esplanade Concert Hall, and also performs regularly at its previous home, the Victoria Concert Hall. The Theatres at Marina Bay Sands feature international headline acts and major musicals.

Theatre works have also become popular and while some are performed at the Arts House and the Theatre Studio at the Esplanade, many are in smaller venues. The wonderful Jubilee Hall at Raffles Hotel has some performances as does the Drama Centre in the National Library Building (100 Victoria Street), and the DBS Arts Centre (20 Merbau Road, near Clarke Quay).

This latter venue is the home of the Singapore Repertory Theatre which in addition to its repertoire of original work has produced a number of Western classics starring Asian performers.

Some films are made in Singapore but Hollywood movies are shown in the many cineplexes found throughout the city. For a different experience you could try the Screening Room (12 Ann Siang Road), an entertainment venue which fuses film, food and nightlife. There are five different levels, each with a different ambiance; two bars, a restaurant, a film theatre and a multi-function events studio. The films are often art-house movies or old favorites such as *The Godfather* and *Casablanca*.

This is not to be confused with a small cinema tucked within the Arts House (1 Old Parliament Lane) with the same name. The Screening Room is an intimate 75-seat film theatre which presents a mix of domestic and international films. The 82-chair Picturehouse (2 Handy Road), housed on the sixth floor in the national heritage site of The Cathay has been airing independent films since the 1990s, however, it was not operating at the time of writing.

**Other useful information**

Mobile phone and internet facilities are excellent and comparable to the best in the world. International roaming services, however, can be very expensive so some visitors prefer to buy a local pre-paid sim card. Text messaging is cheap.

The postal service is efficient and post offices are found throughout the city. The central GPO has poste restante facilities. Post offices open from 8 a.m. to 6 p.m. Monday to Friday and from 8 a.m. to 2 p.m. on Saturday. International courier services operate in Singapore.

Singapore's television and radio channels offer a mix of English, Tamil, Chinese and Malay programs and international satellite channels are available in most hotels. Local newspapers are available in English, and hotels, bookstores and newsstands have a wide range of international publications.

The electricity system is supplied at 220-240 volts so equipment using 110 volts requires an adaptor. These are available from major hotels and in electrical shops. Most wall sockets accommodate the large three-pronged square pin plugs as used in the United Kingdom although some major hotels will have other outlets in their bathrooms.

Singapore is eight hours ahead of Greenwich Mean Time and 13 hours ahead of Eastern Standard Time in the USA.

**Arriving by Air**

Singapore Changi Airport is the main airport in Singapore and a major aviation hub in south-east Asia. It is about 17 km north-east of the commercial centre of the city. There are three passenger terminals and a fourth scheduled for 2017. Terminals 1, 2, and 3 are directly connected via a monorail people mover system. It is the fifth busiest airport by international passenger traffic and one of the busiest cargo airports in the world.

The airport is regularly voted as one of the best in the world and there is a wide array of experiences available within its buildings. There are the usual shops, restaurants, bars and lounges but few airports offer such things as rooftop swimming pool, free foot and calf massage stations, beds in the Rainforest Lounge, and a two-storey enclosed garden with six meter-high waterfall and more than 1000 butterflies.

There are also cactus, orchid and sunflower gardens, free movies at two theatres, a four-storeys high slide, and a 24-hour gymnasium. If you happen to be transiting and have some time, a free two-hour guided tour of Singapore is available.

Getting from the airport to the city is easy. A taxi is the most popular form of travel but you can use public transport. There is a MRT station connected to terminals 2 and 3 where you take a train to Tanah Merah station then transfer to a westbound train to the city. This takes around 30 minutes. Alternatively, bus 36 runs between the airport and the city and departs from the basements of all terminals.

## Getting around

Singapore is a small country but it still takes some mastery to get around. A car can be handy but equally it can be a hassle so most visitors will not opt for this option. Here is my personal take on the situation.

**Walking** is the best way to see an area despite the heat and the possible rain. If you have read the earlier chapters in this book you will know that my sightseeing is based primarily around walking. Don't be fooled into thinking you can walk everywhere, however, and you will need to take taxis or public transport if you want to see more than the area around your hotel.

The **Mass Rapid Transit** (MRT) system is great and my preferred method of travel on the island. Smart, clean air-conditioned trains run both underground and at ground level and provide access to almost every part of Singapore. Trains operate from 5.15 a.m. till mid-night. There is a host of ticketing schemes based on stored value smartcards from one-time travel tickets to tourist concession passes.

Standard value cards are purchased from machines at all stations while stored value cards (ez-link cards) are purchased from ticket offices at selected stations. The Singapore Tourist Pass is a card that allows for unlimited travel on public buses and trains.

It is available as a 1-day, 2-day or 3-day pass and is available from the MRT station at Changi Airport (CG2) and some central city MRT stations such as Orchard (NS22), Chinatown (NE4/DT19), City Hall (EW13/NS25), and Raffles Place EW14/NS26).

You tap the card on a machine as you enter the station then again as you leave. This insures that you only pay for the distance you travel. Smoking, eating and drinking are prohibited on the MRT.

**Buses** are run by two companies and tickets are interchangeable. Buses cover the whole island and once you have a map are relatively easy to use. Bus stops show the route numbers of all buses that stop there but it helps to be familiar with local names. The easiest way to pay is with an ez-link card which you tap against a machine when boarding and leaving a bus.

You can pay by cash on most buses but you need the exact fare as no change is given. Buses run from about 5.30 a.m. to mid-night. Limited Nightrider and Nite Owl services are available after mid-night in the inner city area on Friday and Saturday.

**Taxis** are available 24 hours and are highly regulated so generally service is good. All taxis have meters and fares are quite reasonable but be aware that there are surcharges for Peak Hour, After Mid-night, City Area and there are some other location surcharges. Tips are not expected.

You can hail taxis anywhere but there are certain streets and areas where they cannot stop or wait. In the central city this is any road where there are buses and it applies from 7.30 a.m. to 8 p.m. Monday to Saturday. It is best to get a taxi from one of the numerous taxi stands around the city including at shopping centers and hotels. You can call for a taxi by dialing 6-DIAL-CAB (6342 5222). River taxis operate on the Singapore River with single-trip tickets or a day pass.

Uber is operating in Singapore and there are three types of services: Uber Taxi, which allows users to request and pay for a taxi, like a TransCab or CityCab taxi; UberX, which allows users to book regular private cars; and UberExec, a premium service where you can book a more fancy car like a Mercedes-Benz E-Class. The minimum fare for an UberX ride starts from S$8, while the minimum fare for an UberExec ride starts from S$12.

**Organized tours** are a good way of seeing the city's major sights in relative comfort and there are plenty of companies offering them. Most usually take in the central city, Orchard Road, Chinatown and Little India but others cover specific interests such as World War II sites or evening nightlife. Tours can be by walking, bus, ferry, taxi and even an amphibious Duck.

Some companies which are popular are Journeys Pte Ltd for walking tours (http://www.singaporewalks.com), City Sightseeing for hop on-hop-off tours (Tel: 6338 6877), Viator for bus tours (http://www.viator.com/Singapore-tours/), and River Explorer for boat tours (Tel: 6339 6833).

## Tourist Information

The main **Singapore Visitors Centre** is at 216 Orchard Road (next to orchardgateway@emerald) (Tel:+65 6738 0579). The services and facilities available here are tourist enquiries, customizing of itineraries, booking of tours, sale of attractions and event tickets, hotel reservations, sale of souvenirs, free WIFI, and exhibitions at level 2 of the building. It operates from 9.30 a.m. to 10.30 p.m. The nearest MRT station is Somerset (NS23).

There is another outlet at ION Orchard Level 1 Concierge. This opens from 10 a.m. to 10 p.m. The nearest MRT station is Orchard (NS24). A third outlet has recently opened in Chinatown. This is known as the Chinatown Visitor Centre @ Kreta Ayer Square (2 Banda Street behind the Buddha Tooth Relic Temple and Museum). It operates Monday to Friday, 9 a.m. to 9 p.m. and Weekends and Public Holidays, 9 a.m. to 10 p.m.

The Singapore Tourism Board is a professional organization with much useful information on its website http://www.visitsingapore.com

## Some Unusual Things to Do

You won't find most of these in regular guide books but some of these suggestions can make your visit quite memorable.

**Prawn fishing** in a pool-sized tank sounds pretty easy but it's surprisingly difficult. There are about a dozen places in Singapore where you can catch your dinner with a fishing rod, and then fry it up on a barbecue. At the Banyan Beer Garden at one of these pools (6 Tebing Lane) there is a large LCD flat screen TV to watch live sport while having finger food.

**Bird singing** is big in Singapore. Every morning, groups of mainly men take their birdcages to one of a dozen or so of Singapore's bird singing corners, where they sit around, drink coffee and argue about whose birds are best. On Sunday competition days birds are judged on how well they sing and how they dance.

The Kebun Baru Birdsinging Club meets at Ang Mo Kio near Blk 159 Ang Mo Kio Ave 5 where the birdmen pull their cages up very tall poles onto a hook and there are literally hundreds of cages, and birds warbling in each one. It's a great place to soak up a bit of local culture and also to chat with devoted enthusiasts.

**Monkey Walks** are held around 5 p.m. on the second Saturday of each month by the Jane Goodall Institute at the Bukit Timah Nature Reserve, which is a surprisingly good place for wildlife spotting. You might spot large monitor lizards, a snake or two and red-eared terrapins are common. Monkeys are everywhere.

The group meets around 17:00 at the Bukit Timah Visitor's Centre and begins with a brief classroom session with an introduction about Singapore's long-tailed macaques and a chance to ask any questions.

## Conferences, Conventions and Meetings

Consistently ranked as Asia's Top Convention City by the International Congress and Convention Association, Singapore is a global leader for business events. With at least five first-class convention centers, more than 150 hotels, and around 55,000 hotel rooms, Singapore is my choice for conventions and meetings in the Asia-Pacific region. The great bonus is that its 5.4 million residents are friendly and English is the commonly spoken language.

It is a base for knowledge-driven industries and provides a concentration and variety of activities that is easily accessible and user-friendly. With world-class infrastructure, skilled workforce and strong trade links, Singapore is a choice destination to hold MICE events.

The Singapore Exhibition & Convention Bureau (http://www.yoursingapore.com/content/mice/en.html) has been established to encourage business travel and business events, so it is available to help organizers with their arrangements. In particular it aims to create, grow, and attract business events that reinforce Singapore's reputation as a business and intellectual hub.

While Singapore is the smallest nation in south-east Asia, the IMF ranks it as the third wealthiest country in the world in terms of GDP per capita, thanks to its solid economy. It is also the busiest port in the world and is recognised as the top city in Asia for safety and quality of living.

Singapore has four main meeting and convention centers that cater to tens of thousands of delegates, and several other facilities associated with hotels that can cater for over 1000 delegates.

The **SingaporeExpo** is the city's largest conference center with 10 convention and exhibition halls. There are also 10 Conference Halls, six Meeting Rooms and an Outdoor Open Area. The MAX Pavilion, a multi-purpose event hall with auditorium style seating, has nine meeting rooms and eight conference spaces suitable for break-out sessions, and press rooms.

Singapore EXPO's new convention wing, MAX Atria, provides additional meeting space and 32 meeting rooms. Restaurants and food outlets offer Chinese, Western and Indian food.

The whole complex is located only one MRT stop or 5 minutes by car from the Changi International Airport and within walking distance of two business hotels with 564 rooms; Capri by Fraser at Changi City and Park Avenue Changi Hotels & Suites.

The **Sands Expo and Convention Centre** is the biggest MICE facility in central Singapore. It is part of the Marina Sands complex which includes the city's largest hotel (2561 rooms), the most up-market shopping centre, a large casino, two theatres which play host to the world's best entertainment, the iconic ArtScience Museum and many other facilities.

**Suntec Singapore International Convention and Exhibition Centre** has 31 meeting rooms, four exhibition halls, three ballrooms, three convention halls, and one theatre. Suntec is in the central city and is surrounded by hotels, restaurants and other facilities. There is an adjacent underground MRT station and numerous bus routes connecting to all parts of the city. The Suntec Joint Marketing Alliance offers more than 5,200 hotel rooms within walking distance of the convention centre.

**Resorts World Sentosa Singapore** has over 40 different venue options to choose from including one of south-east Asia's largest, column free ballrooms. The spaces are ideal for big conventions for up to 6,000 people, as well as small incentive groups. It includes six hotels, a large casino, the Universal Studios Singapore theme park, Marine Life Park, and several other attractions. There are 1595 rooms within the Resorts World complex and almost 1500 more outside but still on Sentosa Island.

Elsewhere, **Raffles City Convention Centre** offers another smaller choice within the central city. It consists of a large function space, 27 meeting rooms, and three ballrooms. It is positioned near luxurious Raffles Hotel and it adjoins the Fairmont Singapore and Swissôtel The Stamford hotels.

Outside these convention centers, events can be held at a number of other spaces, including The Meadow at Gardens by the Bay that accommodates up to 30,000 standing people. Also here is the 500-person indoor Waterview Room and the 1,100-person Flower Field Hall. The newly opened Sports Hub with its retractable roof offers other venues such as the 6,000-seat Aquatic Centre & Leisure Water Facility and the 3,000-seat OCBC arena.

City hotels, luxury resorts, historic properties and cute boutique hotels are all available in Singapore. Most hotels offer business centers, meeting rooms, Internet access, and more. Many have quite large meeting and convention facilities so there is enormous choice if you are planning something in Singapore.

# 12 FOOD, DRINK AND NIGHTLIFE

Singaporeans are obsessed with eating and food is a frequent topic of conversation. Locals will queue endlessly, traverse the island, and eat at all hours in order to get the food they want. While there are restaurants everywhere, most Singaporeans prefer humble street fare found in food and hawker centers and coffee shops throughout the island.

Singapore food has Chinese, Indian, Malaysian and Indonesian influences and the cuisine is best defined by, 'it's food you eat in Singapore'.

The fact that there are at least 20,000 eateries to feed a nation of around five million is testament that food is integral to the Singaporean lifestyle. Breakfast is usually eaten at home and lunch tends to be rushed in favor of the working day, but the evening meal is a time to socialize with friends and really enjoy the food.

A meal in most places is judged solely by what comes on the plate and so simple stalls cooking just one dish can be extraordinarily popular. Street food has been popular since the late 1800s, when men from China, Malaya and southern India were drawn to work here. They cooked the dishes they knew from home, selling them on street corners from pots suspended on shoulder poles or from bicycles ingeniously fitted with little portable stoves.

Long before anyone had thought of the label "fusion food", these street vendors were borrowing from each other, unwittingly forging a beguiling food culture. As the city grew in the 1970s, the government saw the vendors as a traffic problem and an eyesore so they relocated them into hawker markets or food centers.

While some atmosphere was lost they still keep the spirit of old Singapore alive in their new surroundings. As a new generation has taken over, there has been a subtle change by reducing the traditionally heavy use of oil and fat and making the food healthier.

Various cuisines are found all over Singapore but visitors should be aware that Muslims do not eat pork and Hindus and some Buddhists do not eat beef or are vegetarian.

Singapore uses both rice and noodles in dishes. Noodles are served stir fried or in soup. Original Malay dishes often have spicy, fishy sambal, sour herbs, and citrus. Heat is provided by the chili paste stirred into broth, or by a side dish of hot sauce. Chinese-inspired noodles are less hot but no less enjoyable. Chinese noodle broths are typically pork-, chicken- or prawn-based.

You'll hear that crab is the national dish, but prawns are used even more. Because Singapore has so little land, most ingredients have to be imported.

Tropical fruit is popular, eaten straight, blended into juice, and used as a topping in a shaved ice dessert. You will find mangosteen, lychee, rambutan, longan and sugar cane. Calamansi lime is used extensively in broths, chili pastes, and drinks.

Herbs and spices are frequently used. Indian curries use a wide variety of spices while Malay dishes can include fruits and herbs and Indonesian ones can also be exotic. Ginger, peppers, and chilies are used extensively.

Visitors should note that smoking is prohibited in dining and entertainment outlets such as pubs, bars, discotheques, lounges and nightclubs including their outdoor refreshment areas. Tipping is discouraged at restaurants as a 10% service charge will be added to your bill.

## Where to Eat

Many people call Singapore a street food paradise but that is not literally true. The government banned hawking in the street decades ago so hawkers are now housed in enclosed Hawker Centers, which are something like food courts.

Most **Hawker Centers** are hot, humid, and frenetic. They're owned by the government and house individual hawkers that usually specialize in a couple of dishes. There are chicken rice guys, noodle specialists and fritter ladies at all of them. Locals will form long queues at their favorite stalls.

All hawker centers are not the same. If you choose a real one that's frequented by locals, you'll find authentic dishes and a warm welcome as a novelty visitor. If you choose one that attracts tourists it's a very different story - touts push you in every direction and there's a sameness about many of the dishes on offer.

The Singapore Tourism Board promotes the Newton Circus Hawker Centre to international visitors but I find it too touristy, overpriced and the stall holders too aggressive. I no longer go there but if you do, check the prices before you order. Many dishes have a fixed price but fish and lobster depend on the size so are subject to scams.

I much prefer the sprawling East Coast Park Lagoon Village (1220 East Coast Parkway) and the Old Airport Road Food Centre (19 Old Airport Road). I used to be a fan of the Maxwell Road Hawker Centre in Chinatown (11 South Bridge Road), but the last time I went there I thought it was tired and dirty. Anthony Bourdain of TV fame gave the Tian Tian Hainanese chicken rice stall here the thumbs up so perhaps I was just unlucky.

Other centers worth trying include the Adam Road Food Center (Junction of Dunearn Road and Adam Road) which was recently upgraded. This is very popular with lunch time crowds and Malay and Indian food dominates. The Chomp Chomp Food Center (Serangoon Garden) has a wide variety of food at a reasonable price.

The Lau Pa Sat Food Center (Boon Tat Street, Shenton Way, Robinson Road) is housed in a lovely 1894 Victorian filigree cast-iron structure. This was originally a wet market but it has now been restored and converted into a food centre. The food is good and the setting sublime.

The refreshed **Chinatown Food Street** (Smith Street) has assembled specialty dishes from the main Chinese dialects and the different races in Singapore, all under one roof. There are street hawker stalls, shophouse restaurants and ad hoc street kiosks, complete with al-fresco dining along the fully pedestrianised street.

Most of the 100 or so stalls have English signs, making it easy to order. A newly constructed high-ceiling glass canopy shelter and a spot cooling system allow diners to enjoy the area regardless of rain or shine.

***Kopitiams*** (coffee shops) are more than just places for coffee—they're cultural institutions for the locals. They are combination coffee house, bar, and neighborhood breakfast joint. Morning snack, lunch and afternoon snack are all served here, along with a hot kopi (coffee) taken with condensed milk, or Kopi-O, a strong black coffee served with sugar. Try a Kaya Toast to go with it if you have the opportunity.

These are particularly popular in housing estates. Singaporeans gather to chat as well as to eat and drink. Coffeehouses are slowly being phased out because they are struggling financially but those that exist provide cheap, good food in a local atmosphere.

***Cze Chas*** are open-air restaurants selling a range of food. There's table service here, and there are not the crowds like at a Hawker Center. They can really be categorized as down-market restaurants but the food is often excellent.

**Food courts**, which are indoors, often in malls, are somewhat similar to hawker centres but are often air-conditioned and have many fast-food outlets. They often focus on comfort and packaging rather than food quality but are convenient when shopping. They tend to be more expensive than hawker centers but some food courts offer Italian, Korean, Thai, Japanese and Greek cuisine.

While most food courts tend to be similar, two in particular have a real charm of their own. Food Republic (Wisma Atria centre, Orchard Road), has been retro-designed in homage to the 1960s heyday of hawker food. The 23 hand-picked restaurant stations and 60s-inspired kiosks curving around the perimeter of the space have been selected for their much-loved signature recipes. Operating hours are 10 a.m. to 10 p.m.

daily.

The second one of interest, Food Trail (30 Raffles Avenue), is near the Singapore Flyer. There are 17 heritage food stalls offering many of the most popular dishes in Singapore. It is somewhat ironic that here they showcase what Singapore street food might have looked like before all the carts were condemned and food makers had to move into the hawker centers. There is great nostalgic atmosphere in the evening and reasonable food.

Then there's the basement food court at the Marina Bay Sands resort where you can spend less than $10 on an excellent meal. Even with 960 seats, you may take some time finding a table.

There are food options all over the city so it is quite easy to find somewhere good. In the Westgate Shopping Centre in Jurong East there are a few food specialty restaurants of note on floor B2. Two that I particularly like are Hajjah Mariam Cafe, which has a good Ambend Daging set for 2 people, (a large Malay plate dish with either Chicken or Beef Rundung and Malay condiments and vegetables), and an outlet of the famous 328 Katong Luksa restaurant.

Behind IKEA in Queenstown, just off Jalan Bukit Merah Road, you can find the ABC Brickworks Market & Food Centre and there is a dessert shop here that the Singapore Prime Minister lines up for. It is called Jin Jin Dessert and the Chendol and Ice Kachang are very good. The Fried Hokkien Prawn Mee from the Tiong Behru Yi Sheng Fried Hokkien Prawn Mee stall is also very good.

The Tiong Bahru Market has some good food and in Eng Hoon Street there are two restaurants of note; the Tiong Bahru Club and the Tiong Bahru Bakery. (A second Tiong Bahru Bakery outlet is in the basement of Raffles City).

In the Chinatown Food Street (Smith Street) there is the Heng Ji Chicken Rice stall which is good and you can try the Geylang Lor 9 Fresh Frog Porridge or the Tiong Bahru Meng Kee Roast Duck. Both are recommended.

There are, of course, full-fledged indoor **restaurants** in Singapore. Like elsewhere they usually specialize in a specific cuisine. They're typically classier operations than any of the others I have mentioned and you'll have a server to help you around the menu. Some provide excellent fine dining and they provide opportunities for the wealthy sector of the public, the tourist and Western expat.

At the top of the heap are restaurants by Joël Robuchon (Hotel Michael, Sentosa Island), who has been awarded the most Michelin stars in the world; one of America's most celebrated chefs, Mario Batali (Osteria Mozza, The Shoppes at Marina Bay Sands); Taiwan-born André Chiang (Restaurant André, 41 Bukit Pasoh Road); and famous Japanese-born chef Tetsuya Wakuda (Waku Ghin , Marina Bay Sands).

Together, they have created an elite class of fine dining restaurants, which combine the best ingredients with world-famous cooking techniques, delivered in some of the most luxurious settings imaginable. Naturally, they don't come cheap.

Restaurant Andre for instance is S$128++ for lunch (Wed & Fri only), S$298++ for dinner (Tues-Sun) while Waku Ghin is S$400 for 10-course degustation menu, and Osteria Mozza has its Chef's Tasting Menu at S$128++, or with wine pairing S$228++

Other places with a good reputation and generally high price are Jaan (level 70, Equinox Complex, Swissotel The Stamford) a French restaurant with an ornate interior and great view; Les Amis (Shaw Centre, 1 Scotts Road), another French restaurant; Iggys (Hilton Hotel, 581 Orchard Road) a highly regarded European restaurant; and Burnt Ends (20 Teck Lim Road), a modern Australian barbecue restaurant in the heart of Chinatown.

A place offering something different is the Ellenborough Market Cafe in the Swissotel Merchant Court. This has a Peranakan buffet and is a great place to try Asam fish and Kueh Pie Tee (a thin and crispy pastry tart shell filled with a spicy, sweet mixture of thinly sliced vegetables and prawns).

True Blue (49 Amenian Street) is another place to try Peranakan food. The restored shophouse is stuffed with quirky antiques and the creamy Rendang, Banana Flower Salad and Chap Chye are delicious. And speaking of bananas, Banana Leaf Apolo (54 Race Course Road) is the real deal in Little India where the food is served on banana leaves. Also here, on Clive Street, I enjoy Mubarak Restaurant where the Tea Tarik is great and the Roti Prata, Fried Chicken and Mutabak is superb.

Of course there are thousands of cheaper restaurants scattered around the city which generally provide adequate food. I must say, however, that despite most Singaporeans thinking they are in a food utopia, I have experience poor service and very ordinary food in a number of places in Chinatown and elsewhere over the years so you need to be a bit selective.

Behind the Raffles Hotel there are two famous Hainanese Chicken Rice Restaurants. The first one is on Seah St and is called Swee Kee and the second one is on Purvis Street and is called Chin Chin Eating House.

In Bugis, there are a few nice options. On Baghdad Street, Kampong Glam Cafe is popular, and on Haji Lane there are two nice options, I am, a local hamburger shop, and Shop Wonderland, a cafe.

Local restaurants where the locals eat are fun to try in Little India. You can get a Tiffin box with vegetarian or meat dishes in several of the side streets off Serangoon Road. Also try the Roti Prata and the Teh Tarik from the roadside cafes. They are a great snack between meals.

**Cafes** have become a growing favorite with the young working crowd. International coffee places like Starbucks, Coffee Bean and Tea Leaf, and Toast Box have become places to hang out with friends. Most cafes serve sandwiches, pizzas, pasta and other Western food.

**Fast-food** is a favorite with children, teenagers, and some visitors. There are McDonald's, KFC, Pizza Hut, Burger King, and MOS Burger outlets everywhere.

The **Changi Airport Staff Canteen** located in Terminal 1, (Level B1) is a secret gem open to the public. There is a lift near the restaurants on the departure floor but it is a bit hidden so you may have to ask someone to direct you.

There are many good local food options there at very good prices compared to the normal airport restaurants. Chicken Rice, Nasi Lemak and Economy Rice are all great choices and you can finish off with an Ice Kachang before the flight.

## What to Eat

**Chicken rice** can be found everywhere and is one of the most popular dishes in the city. Steamed or boiled chicken is served over rice, with sliced cucumber on the side. You can also get roasted chicken served in a similar way. There is always a dipping sauce made from dark soy sauce, chili, garlic and ginger. It is usually accompanied by a bowl of light chicken broth.

**Chili crab** is another favorite and is one of the most requested dishes for visitors. The tangy sauce is made with garlic, chili, tomato and rice vinegar, while flour and egg ribbons are added to give it a fluffy texture.

**Char kway teow** Is a high-fat hawker favorite. It traditionally consists of flat rice noodles stir-fried with lard, soy sauce, chili, cockles, Chinese sausage, bean sprouts, chives and sometimes egg. Now cockles are becoming less common and are being replaces by prawns and some places are reducing the fried pork lard for health reasons.

**Wonton** or Wanton mee is dumplings suspended in noodle soup. Thin egg noodles are used in a well-balanced sauce, with either pork or shrimp dumplings.

**Stingray** with sambal on top is delicious. Sambal is a versatile chili paste blended with spices, shallots, nuts and fermented shrimp paste. The sambal-coated stingray pieces are wrapped in banana leaves and grilled. It is also known as Ikan Bakar (barbequed fish). Lime is usually squeezed in right before eating.

**Carrot cake** (chai tow kuay) is not what most Westerners expect. Rice flour and grated radish is mixed and steamed into large slabs then cut into little pieces and fried with various sauces and vegetables. This grease-laden dish is available at many hawker centers and is popular with the locals.

**Oyster omelet** is a supper favorite for both locals and visitors. Potato starch is mixed into egg batter and oysters are added just before serving. Stalls that sell carrot cake also often sell oyster omelets as it's a similar cooking process.

**Bak kut teh** is a Chinese dish where pork ribs are boiled for hours with garlic, pepper, herbs and spices. It comes either as clear, peppery broth or darker, more herbal stew. A hot pot of Chinese tea helps dissolve the fats in the meaty ribs.

**Fried Hokkien mee** was a dish favored by hardworking laborers and it is still popular. Thick egg noodles mixed with rice vermicelli are cooked in a seafood stock. Prawns, squid, small strips of pork belly, garlic and bean sprouts are then added with some tangy calamansi juice.

**Rojak** is a strange sort of fruit salad. Pieces of fruit, vegetables, dried tofu, fried dough fritters and cured cuttlefish are mixed in a prawn paste sauce and topped with crushed peanuts. The result is a weird mix of flavors which can take some getting used to.

**Popiah** is similar to a non-cooked Chinese spring roll. The soft skin is smeared with a sauce before carrots, bean sprouts, Chinese sausage, shredded omelet and crushed peanuts are wrapped.

**Katong laksa** (Laksa lemak) is thick rice vermicelli in spicy coconut gravy. The soup is often slightly gritty from the ground dried shrimp. The noodles are cut into smaller lengths, so it can be easily eaten with a spoon. Assam laksa, a lighter version of the dish, is served with a tangy fish-based broth.

**Rendang** is beef, chicken or lamb slowly simmered with coconut milk and spices until the meat is tender and the gravy has been absorbed. Lemongrass, galangal, garlic, turmeric, ginger and chillies are pounded into a spice mixture which is used to coat the meat. Coconut milk is then added and it is left to stew for a few hours.

**Yong tau foo** has tofu, vegetables or other items stuffed with fish paste or minced meat paste and served either dry-style or soup-style with a clear broth.

While in China Town you should try the **Bakkwa**, a traditional delicacy at Chinese New Year. The most famous shop for this is Lim Chee Guan on Eu Tong Sen Street.

**Satay** is a kebab-style dish with a few unique twists. The meat is marinated with local spices then put on thin bamboo skewers and grilled over an open charcoal fire. It is often served with chopped raw cucumber and onions, along with rice cakes steamed in coconut leaves. You need to smother the meat with a sweet peanut dip for total enjoyment.

**Ayam penyet** is large pieces of pounded chicken, marinated with many spices, then deep-fried. It's originally Indonesian but has been adopted by Singapore. It is usually served with fried bean curd, soybean cake and vegetables. You can add a delicious sambal belachan relish to provide further flavors.

**Indian mee goreng** is spicy fried noodles with tomatoes, egg, green chilies, mutton mince, cabbage and diced potatoes.

**Curry puffs** are possibly the country's favorite tea-time snack. Traditionally they were filled with curried potatoes, chicken and egg then deep fried but now they also come with all sorts of other fillings.

**Ice kachang** (ice with beans) is ice, served in a bowl or tall glass, covered with creamed corn, condensed milk, and brightly colored syrups. Inside you might find red beans, palm seeds and cubed jellies. Variations are served with fruit cocktail, aloe vera jelly and novelty toppings such as chocolate and durian.

**Durian** is widely regarded by many in Singapore as the 'king of fruits' and it has become the national fruit of Singapore. Most foreigners are turned off by the strong 'pungent' smell, while locals adore the flesh so much they turn it into desserts, cakes, tarts and even shakes.

## What to Drink

**Kopi**, Singapore-style coffee, is served with lots of sweetened condensed milk. If you want it on ice ask for a Kopi-beng. Kopi can be found at every hawker centre, food court, and kopitiam.

**Herbal tea** is often seen in big metal pots outside the traditional medicine shops in Chinatown. The taste can be awful but it is supposed to be good for you. Different teas have different benefits.

**Barley water** is a traditional Chinese drink. You can find it at coffee shops and hawker centers. The taste is mild but the slimy texture is not particularly pleasant.

**Bandung** is a bright pink drink you will find at Malay coffee shops particularly in the Arab Street area. Bandung is a mixture of milk and rose cordial syrup and is sweet and sticky.

**Coconut juice** direct from the coconut or a fresh **lime juice** will go well with most meals and will cool you down. **Sugar cane juice** is produced by a hand-cranked press which squeezes a sweet juice from the cane. It has a very mild flavor but you can add a squeeze of fresh lime to give it some kick.

**Tiger Beer**, a pale lager, has been brewed here since 1932. You can pay S$5 a glass at a hawker centre of S$15 at a Clarke Quay bar for the same thing.

**Craft beer**s have become popular as consumers are more adventurous and willing to try something new. Microbreweries in Singapore have introduced their own craft beer flavors and these have good local following. The first Singapore Craft Beer week was held in 2012 and this has encouraged the trend.

**Singapore Sling** is Singapore's signature cocktail. It is a mix of gin, cherry brandy, pineapple juice, and bitters, garnished with a pineapple wedge and cherry. It is popular with visitors so most bars charge at least S$15 for a glass but if you go to the Long Bar at Raffles Hotel (and I recommend you do) where it was allegedly invented, you will pay at least S$10 more. The sweet, frothy, pink concoction is meant for ladies.

### Where to drink

**The Exchange** (Asia Square Tower One, 8 Marina View) is a grand brasserie and bar and probably the largest in the CBD. With its leather seats and marble tabletop, the place certainly is grand and swanky, but it's a good place for a coffee or meal, or simply an after work drink.

**Level33** is located 33 floors up the Marina Bay Financial Centre Tower 1. This craft-brewery and bar has great views from the seats on the terrace and there is a good bar and dining menu.

**Ku De Ta** (Marina Bay Sands, Tower 3, 1 Bayfront Avenue) has a wonderful view of the Singapore skyline from the observation deck of the iconic Marina Bay Sands Hotel. Drinks aren't cheap (beers $16 onwards; cocktails $20-$30) but you won't forget the ambiance.

**The Penny Black** (26/27 Boat Quay) was supposedly designed and built in the United Kingdom and shipped here piece by piece. It has been a reliable drinking point since 1999. This was the first pub in this area and it is still the place to go for a perfect pint of Old Speckled Hen, to watch British soccer games and to get an authentic serving of fish and chips wrapped in newspaper.

**Molly Malone's** (56 Circular Road) provides an authentic Irish pub experience. This was Singapore's first Irish pub and it has lost none of its lucky charm in the 18 or so years it has been open. The bar was built in Ireland and shipped to Singapore so it carries an aura of authenticity that most other local Irish pubs lack.

**Brewerkz Riverside Point** (30 Merchant Road, Clarke Quay) has been here for 17 years but it continues to launch new brews that are enjoyed by its regulars. It's a good place to start a Clarke Quay evening.

**Fern & Kiwi** (3C River Valley Road, Clarke Quay) is a live band venue featuring New Zealand beers, wines and even cocktails such as the aptly named Kiwi. It is also a good place for a nightcap as house pour drinks drop to S$7 after 2am on weekends.

**Verre Wine Bar** (8 Rodyk Street, Robertson Quay) is one of Singapore's best wine bars. It specializes in French wine with more than 700 different labels and vintages. Wines are available by the glass (S$15-S$19 per glass).

**B28** (28 Ann Siang Rd) has over 100 labels of whisky and this intimate, 35-seat jazz-led basement bar sells most of them by the nip from S$10. Mixing these premium malts even with water is frowned upon here. Classical jazz is played, and there are some live on stage performances from time to time. Complimentary pork sandwiches are served from 5.30 p.m. to 8.30 p.m.

**Empress Bar**, adjacent to the Empress Restaurant at the Asian Civilisations Museum, is a newly-opened bar that has a wonderful panorama of the Singapore River along Boat Quay. You need to try their signature Asian-inspired cocktails like the Beijing Bellini (dry Italian prosecco, lychee wine, lychee nut), or Red Lotus (Absolut vodka, lychee liqueur, cranberry juice).

**TAB** (Orchard Hotel, 442 Orchard Road) is a mid-sized, entertainment venue that plays host to live music concerts, events and a nightly club experience with Club SONAR. Alternating between live music performances and club DJ sets, it features singers, dancers and DJs from all over Asia.

**28 HongKong Street** (unsurprisingly at 28 Hong Kong Street) has been named the Tenth Best Bar in the World so it must have something. It's a deceptively simple space that is dark and airy, with decor limited to marble table tops, wooden furnishings and gold-rimmed mirrors. The excellent staff help make the place what it is.

**The Mad Men Attic Bar** (11 North Canal Road) has decor which has been described as "like industrial chic gone completely wild". The rooftop location is a draw and their spirits are reasonably priced. They make a mean Reubens and the mac-and-cheese balls are great. The rooftop area offers an awesome view with a low-key vibe and it quite often has live music in the outdoor area.

**1 Altitude** (One Raffles Place) has a breathtaking view of the city. During sunset, when the music isn't too loud, it's the perfect place to take in the view, have some wine and chat with your friends. The music ranges from house music to live acoustic performances, so the ambience goes from chilled-out to party scene.

**The Auld Alliance** ( Rendezvous Grand Hotel) has style in spades. Much of the stuff it stocks is very expensive, but as someone said, "being able to sit next to bottles of whiskey that are older than your grandparents is a thrill in itself".

**40 Hands (78 Yong Siak St)** transformed the Tiong Bahru neighborhood into one of the coolest places in town with independent bookshops, small bars and of course coffee. From Friday to Sunday you will normally have to queue here so go on a weekday (closed Monday) for a great coffee or tea when the crowds have mostly gone.

**Canvas Singapore** (20 Upper Circular Road) is one of the best night spots in Singapore with super friendly crews, affordable prices for drinks, and great music. If you're lucky you get to go for their specialty Comedy Nights which are a blast but tickets sell like hot cakes.

**Night time venues**

**Zouk** (17 Jiak Kim Street) is a hugely popular club, which has been compared with some of the best in Europe. It plays mainly House music to a mostly young crowd spun by its seven resident DJs. There are regular live acts from visiting artistes which are an added draw.

There are actually four outlets here: Zouk main room, Velvet Underground, Phuture and Wine Bar. Velvet Underground, Phuture, Zouk have an admission of S$30 for men and S$25 for ladies. The Wine Bar has free entry.

The **Pangaea** (first level of the Southern Crystal Pavilion), which is connected to the Shoppes at the Marina Bay Sands, has an intimate ambience, personalized services and a strict door policy. Like others clubs in the world-wide Pangaea group, Pangaea Singapore club hopes to attract celebrities. Every square meter of Pangaea is literally meant to be danced on including the tables. The cover charge to enter is S$40.

**Kyo** (133 Cecil Street, Keck Seng Tower) has dark earthy tones, wood furniture and bronze wall panels. There are touches of contemporary Japanese-influenced designs, flexibility and minimalism. It is tasteful and has sophisticated music with each night's playlist having a distinct genre and mood from mainstream to R&B and disco. A cover charge of S$20 for ladies, S$25 for men (inclusive 1 drink) is applied on Friday & Saturday from 10 p.m. onwards.

**Attica** (3A River Valley Road) is a New York style bar and club at Clarke Quay. It offers absolutely stunning views of the Singapore River and the magnificent skyline. Four different bar concepts are successfully intertwined into one in the alfresco bar Lilypad, the stylish and sprawling plush sofa lounge, the Balinese greenery courtyard, and the dance club house "Attica Too". A cover charge of S$28 includes two drinks.

**Crazy Elephant** (3E River Valley Road, Clarke Quay) is probably Singapore's Premiere Rock n' Roll Blues Bar. Management is proud that celebrities such as Deep Purple, R.E.M, Robbie Williams and Ronan Keating have all played here. Live performances start from 10 p.m. every night. The bar is quite small and very crowded on Fridays and Saturdays. Sunday nights is a blues rock jam session when music starts around 8.30 p.m.

**Jazz@Southbridge** (82B Boat Quay) is in a pastel blue vintage building at the corner of South Bridge Road. This is one of the best and authentic Jazz bars in Singapore. The resident jazz band performs nightly and the bar also offers some of the best touring session musicians from around the world. There is a relaxed atmosphere in the cozy interior with comfortable armchairs. Mostly there is no cover charge.

**Other night time activities**

If you are desperate to get away from the concrete city, paths at the **Singapore Botanic Gardens** wind past grassy slopes, towering rain trees, statues and fountains and are open until mid-night. (See chapter 5 for more details). **Gardens by the Bay** is open until 2am for strolling and there are Garden Rhapsody Shows at 7:45 p.m. and 8:45 p.m. (See chapter 4 for more details).

**Night Safari**, the world's first night zoo allows you to see 900 nocturnal animals from 130 species in naturalistic habitats. It is open until mid-night. (See chapter 8 for more details).

**Skypark** at the Marina Sands Hotel is a top viewpoint. It is worthwhile getting a ticket in the very late afternoon to take photographs during the daytime and then wait until darkness falls, so you can see the transformation. The **Singapore Flyer** opens until 10 p.m. providing some excellent night-time views of the city. (See chapter 4 for more details).

Thrill seekers looking for a quick jolt of adrenaline should head down to

Clarke Quay, where the **G-Max Reverse Bundy** will provide a mix of fun and fear. You are fired 60 meters into the air at a speed of up to 200 km/h.

**Hai Bin Prawning** in Bishan provides a lay-back experience and if luck is on your side, a plate of fresh prawns. A thatched roof with hanging red lanterns surrounds six ponds filled with live prawns and fishing equipment and bait are included in the hourly fee, along with barbecue pits, charcoal, satay sticks and salt for seasoning.

Massage is popular in Singapore and **Aramsa's** unusual location in the middle of suburban Bishan Park makes it a great place to visit. 17 Individual spa suites with outdoor showers or baths are linked via resort-style covered walkways. It operates until 10 p.m. early in the week and 11 p.m. on Friday to Sunday. There are many other massage places and spas (some very up-market) in different areas of the city.

Many are in the top hotels and are quite expensive, however, the experience is usually first class. The Spa at Four Seasons Hotel Singapore has a Jet Lag Recovery treatment at S$185 for 60 minutes. The Heavenly Spa by Westin on the 35th floor of the Westin Singapore has a Detox Massage at S$220 for 90 minutes. LifeSpa at 111 Somerset Road has a Body Massage + Anti-Ache Therapy at S$245 for 80 minutes.

**Casinos** have become big business in Singapore. Both Marina Bay Sands and Resorts World Sentosa have table games and slot machines with a selection of the newest and most popular electronic game machines. Both operate 24/7. As a foreign visitor you get free admission if you have your passport with you. Inside some drinks are free.

If you need a sweet treat Holland Village's **2am Dessert Bar** (21a Lorong Liput) offers sleek, modern desserts paired with a carefully selected wine list. Try the smoked white chocolate with hibiscus jelly and cinnamon beads, or the alpaco chili chocolate. It opens from 3 pm to 2 am and after midnight the line can be up to 45 minutes long.

**Actors** (13A-15A South Bridge Rd) can provide you with five minutes of fame by making every spot in their friendly house band free for rock-star wannabes. While the rest of the bars in Singapore have talented resident live bands who entertain the audience, in Actors, the customers are the stars.

Culture vultures are well catered for in Singapore these days. **Esplanade Theatres on the Bay** is a hub for performing arts with a concert hall that seats 1,600, a theatre with a capacity of 2,000, an outdoor performance space and a roof terrace. The Singapore Symphony Orchestra performs weekly concerts here for much of the year. The **Singapore Conference Hall** (7 Shelton Way) is home to the Singapore Chinese Orchestra, the national Chinese orchestra.

Drama and musical theatre can also be found at the Marina Bay Sands Theatre, the 1,700-seat Kallang Theatre, and the lovely Victoria Theatre and Victoria Concert Hall. Programs are available on line and in local tourist publications. SISTIC sells tickets to events ranging from pop concerts, to musicals, theatre, family entertainment and sports. See http://www.sistic.com.sg

The **Chinese Theatre Circle** (5 Smith St.) presents the Sights & Sounds of Chinese Opera with English subtitles every Friday & Saturday. The two options are from 7 p.m. to 9 p.m. where you can enjoy a set Chinese dinner and Chinese tea and dessert for S$40.00 per person or from 8 p.m. to 9 p.m. when Chinese tea, snacks and dessert is available for S$25.00 per person while you watch the show.

# 13 SHOPPING

Singaporeans love to shop. It is no surprise then, to find the city is alive with shopping opportunities. Here are a few suggestions.

## Shopping areas

**Orchard Road** has long been a shopper's paradise and it continues to be a centre for up-market style. There are department stores and shopping malls over a two kilometer length and it is easy to spend several days exploring the options.

**Marina Bay** is now challenging Orchard Road as the style centre due to the huge centers that have been built there in recent years. The Shoppes at Marina Bay Sands sets new heights for stylish shopping.

For vintage and ethnic shopping you should try **Haji Lane**, parallel to Arab Street in Kampong Glam. There you'll find rows of tiny boutiques loaded with all sorts of local goodies at attractive prices. It can be quite a treasure hunt and it's not certain what you will find.

Singapore's **Chinatown** has souvenir stalls, religious offerings, traditional Chinese medicine shops and night-time hawkers. The Ann Siang Road neighborhood on the eastern edge of Chinatown is a mix of designer fashion boutiques, French patisseries and niche bookstores. The area is a maze of lanes lined with delightful old shophouses and makes for a delightful afternoon stroll.

It's messy and loud but **Little India** draws everyone from backpackers to locals on a shopping expedition. With art galleries, un-scrubbed restaurants and vegetable stalls all nicely crammed into small spaces, Little India is a must see on any tourists' circuit even though it may be limited on what you want to buy.

Everyone who has run out of time goes to Mustafa Centre for last-minute shopping and purchases. It's open 24 hours and sells everything from groceries to shampoo, to ethnic jewelry, to the latest electronics.

**Holland Village** is a popular shopping and dining destination for younger Singaporeans and expatriates. It is a mix of shophouses and small malls near the Holland Road and Holland Avenue intersection. There are art and craft shops, street cobblers, novelty shops, gourmet takeaways, wine cellars, body waxing specialists, and tarot card readers, giving it a 'Bohemian' atmosphere.

**Changi Airport** has over 350 retail and service outlets located across three terminals. You will find local food products, electronic gadgets, watches, beauty products, luxury brands, and more here. Passengers departing from Singapore can also enjoy tax-free shopping at the airport without worrying about GST refunds.

**Department stores**

**Robinsons** is a one-stop shopping destination that's well-regarded in Singapore, thanks to its 150-year heritage. It has products for both the affluent shopper and the more price-conscious consumer, offering fashion, homeware, bed linen, sports gear and beauty products. There is a store in the heart of Orchard Road, at Raffles City in the Colonial Centre and JEM in Jurong East.

**Tangs** (310 Orchard Road) focuses on fashion, with brands like French Connection, Studio Tangs and Island Shop. Tangs is targeted at sophisticated and up-market shoppers. Founded in 1932, Tangs has two stores in Singapore, on Orchard Road and at VivoCity.

**Takashimaya** (391 Orchard Road) is a Japanese retailer with an up-market department store catering to the more affluent consumer. It has restaurants offering Chinese, Korean, Indonesian, Thai, Japanese and international dishes, a spa, slimming services, boutiques, a gym, drycleaners, and an art gallery.

It sells sportswear, arts and crafts, ladies fashion from Armani, Burberry, Kenzo, and DKNY, hair and beauty, books, children's, cosmetics, home décor and music.

**Metro** (Paragon, 290 Orchard Rd) has all the usual retail items at prices often less than other department stores. Metro has a flagship store at Paragon as well as stores at Centrepoint, Tampines, Woodlands and Sengkang. The Paragon store is fashion-focused and it has a large shoe department.

**Isetan** (Shaw House, 350 Orchard Road) is a Japanese department store with several branches across Singapore. Isetan is particularly popular because of its huge range, fair prices and good service. It sells just about everything – from perfume, men's, women's and children's fashion, furniture, luggage, sports gear, to electronics, household items, appliances, kitchenware and stationery.

As well as Shaw House, there are stores at Wisma Atria, Katong and at Tampines. Some stores have a supermarket and restaurants.

**OG** started life as a manufacturing factory called Ocean Garments. It opened a store in People's Park in 1970 and now operates three outlets, including OG Orchard and the Albert Complex store. It offers value-for-money clothing, but is slowly moving up market. The OG Orchard shop has a Starbucks cafe, a ramen shop and a steamboat restaurant, while its other two stores also have restaurants.

**John Little** was established in 1845, and is the oldest department store in Singapore. These days the John Little chain is owned by Robinsons. There are currently three stores at Marina Square, Tiong Bahru Plaza and Jurong Point.

There are currently eight **Marks & Spencer** stores in Singapore located at The Centrepoint, Wheelock Place, Parkway Parade, Raffles City, Paragon, Plaza Singapura, VivoCity and Great World City. The stores offer a range of men's and women's fashion, lingerie, frozen meals, confectionaries, fine wines, beauty products, and toiletries. The Robinson Group manages Marks and Spencer in Singapore.

**Malls and shopping centers**

**VivoCity** (1 Harbourfront Walk Telok Blangah Rd.) is Singapore's largest retail and lifestyle destination. You are likely to visit here as it is located just across from Sentosa Island. Its shopping outlets cover fashion, books, electronics, sport, lifestyle, fashion and more.

Note the series of artworks throughout the complex and there is an open-air playground for the kids and a rooftop amphitheatre. The

Harbourfront MRT station is part of the complex.

**ION Orchard** (2 Orchard Turn at Paterson Rd.) has over 330 stores on eight levels. It is one of Singapore's newest and most modern retail centers. It sells some of the world's most exclusive brands and has six flagship stores: Cartier, Louis Vuitton, Prada, Dior, Giorgio Armani and Dolce & Gabbana. There is a large gallery space for its dedicated art program. The Orchard MRT Station (NS22) is accessible directly through the basement.

**The Shoppes at Marina Bay Sands** has a wonderful design and some of the world's best labels. Among the list of retailers here are Bally, Bulgari, Burberry, Cartier, Christian Dior, Fendi, Gucci, Hugo Boss, Prada, Ralph Lauren, Tiffany & Co., Yves Saint Laurent and many others. There is a skating rink, as well as a canal where you can take a relaxing boat ride.

**Suntec City** is located at Marina Centre. This was the largest Singapore Shopping Mall until VivoCity was built. It is linked with the Convention and Exhibition Hall and is divided into four zones: Galleria offering high-end international labels; Tropics offers a more wide-ranging choice of outlets for a wider budget range; Entertainment Centre; and Fountain Terrance. Operating hours are 10 a.m. to 10 p.m. The nearest MRT Station is City Hall (EW13/NS25).

**Paragon** (Orchard Road) is an up-market shopping centre with much appeal. Many branded goods are sold here in stores such as Gucci, Alfred Dunhill, and Escada. Anchor tenants include Metro and Marks and Spencer. The city ticket office for Singapore Airlines is also located here. Operating hours are 10 a.m. to 11 p.m. The nearest MRT stations are Somerset (NS23) or Orchard (NS22)

**Marina Square** is located next to the bay area. There are many fashion boutiques here and the John Little department store. It is connected to City Hall MRT station via the CityLink Mall. Operating hours are 10 a.m. to 11 p.m.

**Ngee Ann City** in Orchard Road is better known to locals as Takashimaya which is the anchor tenant. The Kinokuniya bookstore and the largest Best Denki in Singapore are two of the many stores in here. There is an underpass to Wisma Atria and Lucky Plaza. Operating hours are 10 a.m. to 11 p.m. The nearest MRT Station is Orchard (NS22).

**FestiveWalk at Resorts World Sentosa** has numerous luxury retail outlets. Luxury Fashion has some exclusive brands that have made a debut here include leading Italian jeweller Damiani, Italian luxury menswear label Canali, and Vie Beaute, a modern and interactive beauty hall where you'll find all the major fragrance and cosmetics brands. A further attraction is the first store in Asia for Victoria's Secret.

**Sim Lim Square** (1 Rochor Canal Road) is where the locals go to satisfy their high-tech cravings. Its six levels of computer-related shops with hundreds of electronics dealers offer some of the best prices in Singapore. The customer service leaves a lot to be desired but price is the priority here and competition is fierce, so browse around to compare prices. The better bargains are found on the top floors.

**AMK Hub** (53 Ang Mo Kio Avenue 3) is in the centre of Ang Mo Kio and there are over 200 shops across four levels. There is a bus interchange on Level 1, NTUC Fairprice Xtra, one of Singapore's biggest hypermarkets in the basement and an eight-screen cinema operated by Cathay on the top floor. Small boutique shops are scattered throughout the complex to cater to different groups.

**Velocity @ Novena Square** (238, Thomson Road) is just two MRT stations away from town (Novena MRT NS20) but yet it has its own distinct feel. It calls itself "Singapore's first-ever dedicated sports and lifestyle Mall," and sports and fitness buffs would have a field day here, from the huge gym run by California Fitness to niche boutique shops stocking the latest sports fashion and fitness equipment. The mall also regularly hosts sporting events both indoors and outdoors.

**Golden Mile Complex** (5001 Beach Rd) is Singapore's Little Thailand. It has over 400 shops, and you'll find CDs, beer, fashion and a Thai band at night. There are many outlets with cheap and tasty Thai food and buses from here connect with Malaysia.

## Markets

Malls have virtually taken over from markets in Singapore for everything except food so pickings are rather bleak. The exception is the vibrant

**Chinatown Street Market** (Pagoda, Trengganu and Sago streets) where you can find dragon candles, street opera masks, traditional clothing and Chinese calligraphy and the usual tourist offerings.

There are more than 200 market stalls lining the streets, all of which offer a wide selection of old and new collectibles. The Chinatown Street Market is especially vibrant and fun to visit during traditional holidays such as the Chinese New Year.

**Bugis Street** has become a large retail shopping destination with almost 800 shops in a market-type atmosphere. There are shops offering chic and fashionable clothing and accessories, beauty services like manicure parlors and hair salons, and much more is a buzzing location.

The only daily flea market that I have found is the **Thieves Market** (along Jalan Besar near Sungei Road). It might come across as a step back into the 1950s for the wandering tourist, but it's still popular with some people. Here an assortment of goods from dial telephones, cassette tapes, cooking pots, and broken-but-somehow-still-functioning electronic gadgets is laid out on plastic mats. It can be fascinating to browse through some vanishing gems from a time past.

If you are in Singapore on a Sunday the **China Square Central Weekend Flea Market** (China Square Central, 18 Cross Street) has a mishmash of DVDs, souvenirs and electronics. It opens from 11 a.m. to 6 p.m. Level 2 is home to a couple of comic book stores that stock the latest issues and action figure collectibles.

The **MAAD Market** (Market of Artists and Designers) at the Red Dot Museum, 28 Maxwell Road is held on the first Friday of every month, 5 p.m. to midnight. The family-friendly, pet-friendly and budget-friendly MAAD market is a booming platform for independent people to exhibit, perform, sell, shop and experiment.

As far as innovation goes, this is one of Singapore's best flea markets. Here you'll find an amazing range of crafts, from plush toys, through paintings to hand-made jewelry.

## What to buy

The best time of year to go shopping in Singapore is during the Great Singapore Sale, where retailers offer substantial discounts. The Great Singapore sale begins in June and lasts until July and it attracts large crowds of shoppers arriving from neighboring countries.

When shopping at department stores and in most malls, prices are generally fixed and bargaining is discouraged but in the markets and at smaller retailers be sure to haggle the price as most vendors will accept a lower price than the one initially offered to get a sale.

**Asian antiques and artifacts** are high on the list for many visitors. Fortunately, with imports arriving from most Asian countries and having a rich and ancient history of its own, Singapore offers plenty of treasures. Try the Tanglin Shopping Centre (Orchard Road), Chinatown and Holland Village for good buys.

**Electronic** items are always popular but I don't believe prices and variety is as good here as Hong Kong. Peninsula Plaza is a good place to buy electronics, as are Sim Lim Square (1 Rochor Canal Road) and Funan Digitalife Mall (109 North Bridge Road). Portable DVD players, mobile phones, hi-tech cameras, MP3 players and laptops are up for grabs.

Prices are cheaper than at most other commercial outlets but service is not necessarily great. Serious bargaining and cash can save a few extra dollars.

**Inexpensive clothing** comes as Chinese imitations, brand name surpluses and dead-stocks. Mustaffa Centre, in Little India and some of the shops along Serangoon Road and its offshoots, are good places to look but do not expect to find any sensational bargains. Lucky Plaza on Orchard Road and Far East Plaza, on Scotts Road are other options.

Queensway Shopping Centre (near Alexandra Hospital) has cheap sports gear, limited edition shoes, and sporting apparel. Thousands of shops across the metropolis specialize in international brands but it is probably best to stick to the well-known outlets in the malls and department stores.

Handcrafted **watches** and affordable standard watches can be found in every shopping district of Singapore. The outstanding Cortina Watch Espace in Millenia Walk closed down in 2014 and there was no replacement at the time of writing. Good watch shops can be found in The Shoppes at Marina Bay Sands, Raffles City and Paragon.

**Decoration items** and curios for the home such as statues, wall decorations, paper kites and parasols, calligraphy, posters and other artworks are always popular.

**Chinese herbal medicines** are widely available in Chinese clinics and you will find hundreds of Chinese health shops in Singapore. These drugs are based on ingredients used in China for health care and treatment of wounds. The best place to check out these is Chinatown.

The range of **jewelry** from inexpensive bangles to million-dollar crown jewels is simply mind-boggling. There are many gold jewelry shops lined along Serangoon Road near the Little India MRT Station (NE7), and at Mustafa Centre.

When buying expensive jewelry, the QJS emblem (Quality Jewelers of Singapore) will give you some confidence. Many items have fixed retail prices based on weight, purity and craftsmanship. If you buy something, make sure you obtain an invoice indicating the fineness, weight and price of the item.

The orchid is the Singapore national flower and 24 karat **gold plated real orchids** are interesting buys. These flowers can be bought from Risis stores.

Singapore produces its own **perfumes** which are extremely low in price and have interesting aromas.

# 14 ACCOMMODATION

Singapore currently has around 55,000 visitor rooms in a multitude of hotels and other accommodation. Occupancy rates are around 85% so price pressure is small and the average hotel room last year cost nearly S$275. The number of hotels continues to grow each year so the choice is becoming wider and niche markets are being filled. It is the mid-market area which is growing strongest.

Some of the top hotels are amongst the best in the world while there is a good choice of 3 and 4-star properties, some of which are extremely funky properties in recycled old buildings. The area you chose depends somewhat on what you plan to do but provided the accommodation is near a MRT station it is not particularly critical. The following are personal selections.

**Raffles Hotel Singapore** ***** 1 Beach Road; http://www.raffles.com/singapore/

It's great to visit the restaurants and bars but to actually stay and experience this world-famous classic hotel is something else. It is an oasis of colonial style, calm and charm in the heart of modern Singapore. The 103 suites are quiet, have Oriental carpets on teakwood flooring, 24-hour butler service, dressing area and en-suite bathroom with separate walk in shower and bathtub, and every other amenity you are likely to need.

The high ceilings and generous size give you room to breathe. Service is spectacular. Everything exudes old-world charm and class yet the staff are friendly, helpful and courteous.

Dining options are the Bar & Billiard Room, Raffles Grill, Tiffin Room with its curry buffet, Long Bar Steakhouse, Raffles Courtyard, Ah Teng's Bakery, Long Bar the home of the Singapore Sling, the Writers Bar, and the Martini Bar. Raffles Spa with its 6 private treatment rooms, sauna and steam room, and Jacuzzi and outdoor swimming pool is exclusively for the use of guests.

**Capella Singapore** ***** 1 The Knolls, Sentosa Island; http://www.capellahotels.com/singapore/

The hotel is located on Sentosa Island so it is not great if you need to spend most of your time on the main island but Resort World and Universal Studio are within walking distance for shopping, dining and entertainment. It is, however, a perfect place to unwind and relax in a property with stylish design and fantastic staff. Curved, modern buildings gently intermingle with colonial classics and the verdant, rainforest. The hotel is famed for its personalized service.

There are three main pools and the garden villas each have a plunge pool. The Library is a wonderful place to enjoy a good book or a great conversation. Chinese cuisine is available at Cassia, Mediterranean at The Knolls and you can unwind after a long day at Bob's Bar. Auriga Spa has nine experience rooms with private gardens.

**The Ritz-Carlton, Millenia Singapore** ***** 7 Raffles Avenue; http://www.ritzcarlton.com/en/Properties/Singapore/

The Marina Bay view is just awesome and you can soak in the bath while enjoying the night view. This is a large hotel with 608 guest rooms and facilities to match. The lobby is gorgeous and the large pool good for doing laps.

Dining choices include Summer Pavilion with classical, Cantonese delicacies; Greenhouse, an all-day international restaurant; Shiraishi with Japanese cuisine; and the Chihuly Lounge with traditional afternoon tea, cocktails and bar bites, and live entertainment in the evening. Behind the hotel is a shopping mall which gives many further choices.

Club guests can access the Club Lounge, located on the 32nd floor and enjoy a champagne breakfast, mid-day light refreshments, three-tiered classic afternoon tea, hors d'oeuvres and cocktails, and desserts with cordials.

**The Fullerton Bay Hotel Singapore** ***** 80 Collyer Quay; http://www.fullertonbayhotel.com/

This is a superb hotel with heaps of style and class providing a relaxing sanctuary along the bay. The location is great and the rooms are stylish with fantastic views and good size. Polished rosewood and latticed screens, and leather and chrome, help the elegant and refined atmosphere in the bedrooms.

Dining options include Clifford, a French American brasserie with true waterfront dining; The Landing Point with its 13-metre long bar serves organic salads, sandwiches, local Asian favourites, and afternoon tea; The Clifford Pier preserves hawker culture by serving Singapore delicacies and reinterpretations of Asian specialties and Western classics; and Lantern, a stylish rooftop bar and pool which serves gourmet snacks, accompanied with fine champagnes, signature cocktails, wines and beverages.

The Fullerton Bay connects via an air conditioned subway to its nearby sister hotel, The Fullerton. This considerably expands the food and beverage offerings.

**Shangri-La Hotel Singapore** ***** 22 Orange Grove Road; http://www.shangri-la.com/singapore/shangrila/

Set amidst 15 acres of lush greenery, Shangri-La Hotel Singapore is consistently voted as one of the best hotels in the world. There are guestrooms and suites in three distinctive wings, serviced apartments and residences in four-storey villas. Although it is a large hotel there is a warm atmosphere unlike some of the modern cold places.

It has large rooms and bathrooms, very nice swimming-pool areas and excellent food in the various restaurants such as The Waterfall, The Line, Nadaman Japanese Restaurant, or Shang Palace.

At night you can relax in the Lobby Court with musical entertainment or unwind in the quiet gardens. Rooms have a complicated electronic control system for turning lights on and off which is annoying to some guests.

The Valley Wing which is the high end of the hotel has its own private entrance, butler, and silver service breakfast room. Complimentary French champagne is served in the evenings in the foyer.

**Marina Bay Sands** ***** 10 Bayfront Avenue, Marina Bay; http://www.marinabaysands.com/

Towering over the bay, this iconic hotel offers luxury with an amazing 2530 rooms, 20 dining options and a world-class casino. Rooms are fitted with modern dark wood furnishings, flat-screen cable TVs, carpeted floors, iron/ironing board, safe deposit box, and some have iPod dock and coffee machine. Stunning views of the Singapore skyline can be enjoyed from floor-to-ceiling windows.

Set on top of three towers, a Sky Park features landscaped grounds, an observation deck, a spectacular infinity pool, world-renowned Banyan Tree Spa, and two restaurants. There are some exclusive fine dining restaurants, a dance club, three lounges and all sorts of facilities in a giant shopping mall.

**The Forest by Wangz** **** 145A Moulmein Road; http://forestbywangz.com/

This boutique serviced apartments is architecturally stunning with bold designer furniture and vibrant sculptures in every apartment. There is a choice of studio or one-bedroom apartments each with a fully-equipped kitchenette. Complimentary internet, local calls, breakfast and parking are included. The infinity-edge lap pool features a shallow lounging area and there is a well-equipped gym.

The Residents Lounge promotes communal activities, entertainment and exchanging of ideas while the Rooftop Deck provides nice views across the Singapore skyline. Washing and dryer facilities in the building are a convenient touch. It is situated in a residential area, just a few minutes' walk from a bustling new commercial district, and the Novena MRT Station (NS20) is just 5 minutes on foot.

**Amoy** **** 76 Telok Ayer Street; http://www.stayfareast.com/en/hotels/amoy/

This is a beautiful boutique hotel just 400 meters from Chinatown MRT Station (NE4/DT19). The rooms over three floors are beautifully designed and furnished, with super-comfortable beds and crisp white bed linen. They have interiors that evoke the charm of traditional Chinese design and architecture as well as the comfort and convenience of contemporary facilities.

Rooms have slippers, bathroom scales, an iron and ironing board, a room safe, hairdryer etc. The air-conditioning is quiet and efficient; the complimentary mini-bar and the nibbles are replenished daily. It offers free Wi-Fi access, free breakfast spreads and free shuttle services from Changi International Airport. There is first-class service from a small but dedicated team.

**The Quincy Hotel** **** 22 Mount Elizabeth; http://www.stayfareast.com/en/hotels/the-quincy-hotel

The 108 room Quincy Hotel, located close to Orchard Road and the botanic gardens, offers the best that technology has to offer whilst maintaining a quirky edge. It has stylish all-inclusive studios with free Wi-Fi, iPod docking station, cable TV, laptop safe, mini bar, coffee/tea maker, and iron/board. There is a 24-hour fitness centre, and an infinity glass pool overlooking the city.

Guests can enjoy a one-way airport shuttle service and complimentary refreshments. Breakfast and all day light refreshments are offered at the lobby restaurant. Quincy has recently introduced complimentary Art Jamming sessions for couples. On weekends, you can also indulge in romantic movies that are screened by the pool.

**One Farrer Hotel & Spa** **** 1 Farrer Park Station Road; http://www.onefarrer.com/

This is an urban resort situated in Singapore's Little India district next to Farrer Park MRT station. There are 243 rooms, suites and villas covering a diverse range of accommodation. The Spa Retreat houses a Holistic Spa, Aesthetic Spa, and a host of relaxing pleasures to ease your mind and body, including Japanese-style onsens, reflexology water walks, and an Olympic-size swimming pool.

Escape is a 24-hour restaurant while Flip Flop, serves classic comfort food, grilled specialties and spa cuisine by the pool. Sunset Bar provides breathtaking sunsets as you sip on your favorite cocktail.

**Holiday Inn Orchard City Centre** **** 11 Cavenagh Road; http://www.holidayinn.com/hotels/us/en/singapore/

The hotel is conveniently located in the heart of the city, a two-minute walk from Orchard Road. The modern rooms are equipped with flat-screen cable TVs, DVD players, mini-bars and tea/coffee makers. All rooms have internet access and complimentary newspaper delivery is available.

Restaurant choices are the award-winning Indian restaurant, Tandoor, or Asian and International cuisines at the Window on the Park Restaurant. There is a rooftop pool and a fitness centre. For a more pampering stay, upgrade to an executive club room and enjoy access to the exclusive club lounge with privileges like complimentary breakfast and cocktails.

**Naumi Hotel** **** 41 Seah St.; http://www.naumihotel.com/

The central city location is ideal if you want to go shopping at places like Raffles City, Suntec City and Bugis Junction or simply chill out at CHIJMES. A Singapore partner of Small Luxury Hotels, the 73 room boutique hotel has garnered a range of awards over the past few years. The Table Restaurant & Bar is sexy with swanky décor and signature cocktails. Table by Rang Mahal has style and will transport you to the streets of India.

There are three gyms dedicated to cardio and weights, and the rooftop infinite edge pool is pure bliss. Microsoft Xbox 360 and Nintendo Wii gaming consoles are available for loan on a complimentary basis. There is a dedicated ladies floor and the guest rooms here have special products and complimentary benefits.

**Parkroyal on Pickering** **** 3 Upper Pickering St; http://www.parkroyalhotels.com/Pickering/

This environmentally friendly hotel provides guests with a natural environment of hanging gardens and lush greenery whilst maintaining

5-star comfort and service. Public spaces are airy while rooms are efficiently designed and are walled by floor-to-ceiling windows, but are quite small. The pool area is a nice retreat, the gym is huge and fully equipped, and the lush sky garden is a great space for a jog.

The business lounge is very intimate, relaxing, and it also serves delicious cakes and great coffee. Lime restaurant serves a mix of Asian and international flavors. The spa has a choice of signature treatments, traditional therapies, facials, baths and massages. Club room facilities are great value for money with champagne breakfasts, afternoon tea from 2 p.m.to 4 p.m. each day and cocktails and some hot food from 6 p.m.to 8 p.m.

**New Majestic** **** 31-37 Bukit Pasoh; http://www.newmajestichotel.com/

The 30-room funky hotel is a modern fit-out of an old building. It has gorgeous styling and art but will be short on comfort for some people. Each room is different and equipped with vintage as well as designer furniture. Some of the rooms are attic-styled rooms with beds you reach by climbing a ladder. Some rooms have dual his-and-hers cast iron bath tubs which are perfect for a couple's getaway.

The hotel is built around a courtyard with a small swimming pool, and some rooms overlook this area, giving a private garden atmosphere. Rooms contain a Nespresso in-room coffee maker, Kiehl's toiletries, a Samsung smart TV and Ploh bedding and bath robes. Soft drinks and water in the mini-bar are complimentary. It is just a minute's walk to the Outram Park MRT station (EW16/NE3).

**Wanderlust Hotel** *** 2 Dickson Road; http://wanderlusthotel.com/

This is another quirky, designer hotel which will appeal to those who don't like conventional large, modern properties. It is located in Little India and the building was originally an old school built it 1920s. They have amazing themed rooms on four levels which are spotless and good value with massive showers and comfortable beds. Many are small and brightly colored so you should look before you buy.

There is an eclectic foyer full of cluttered objects which is lots of fun and Cocotte restaurant serves up unpretentious, rustic French cuisine in a casual and comfortable setting. The unusual hotel is just minutes walk to one of the more interesting areas of Singapore.

**Kam Leng Hotel** *** 383 Jalan Besar; http://www.kamleng.com/

The hotel was first established in 1927 and it was remodeled and re-opening in 2012. It invokes a sense of nostalgia as it recreates the mood and style of the original while providing modern amenities. From the outside the four-storey hotel looks like something of a time warp, and in fact the interior has retained a lot of its original features, which adds to the overall character.

The design of each of the 70 rooms is highly influenced by Peranakan style. The breakfast is good and immediately across the road is a 24 hr food court. The staff are friendly but there are few general facilities. The location is convenient, with a bus stop just across the road, and the MRT station is about 10 minutes walk away.

**Holiday Inn Express Clarke Quay** *** 2 Magazine Road; http://www.ihg.com/holidayinnexpress/hotels/us/en/singapore/

The hotel is modern with 442 rooms arranged around an open-air atrium with unenclosed hallways. The rooms are smartly planned, have floor-to-ceiling windows, are clean and comfy but are fairly small. They have universal power points and the Wi-Fi is quick and free. There is a mini-garden on level four and the rooftop garden, pool and gym on the roof is a great asset.

There is a respectable breakfast buffet in the Great Room but other meals are not available. The convenient coin laundry, ice machines and drink vending machines will be welcomed by many. The Hotel is walking distance to Chinatown and Clarke/Boat Quay.

**Hotel Kai** ***14 Purvis St; http://www.hotelkai.com

The hotel has converted a Purvis Street shophouse into a series of personal cabins. While small, they are urban and comfortable cocoons to rest in after a long day walking around the nearby Colonial District. Sizes vary from 6 square meters (minute) to 35 square meters (larger than most hotel rooms in Singapore). It has its own bistro which serves gourmet burgers and craft beers and free bottled water, snacks, coffee and tea making facilities are provided daily.

**Jayleen 1918 Hotel** *** 42 Carpenter Street; http://www.jayleen1918.com.sg/

The location is excellent, one street back from the river and 100 m from shops, restaurants, pubs, MRT, buses etc. The rooms are small but have everything you need for a short stay but be aware that some do not have windows. Facilities include a flat-screen TV, air-conditioning with individual settings, rain showers, hair dryer and toiletries, mini bar with soft drinks and tea, coffee and drinking water. Rates include a limited breakfast. The roof-top patio is pleasant.

**Hotel 1929** *** 50 Keong Saik Road; http://www.hotel1929.com/

The hotel is in a beautiful restored building in Chinatown. The 32 rooms, although cleverly designed and stylish, are very small and noise is a problem in some. The shower and toilet are together in the bathroom with the basin on the outside. Rooms are air-conditioned and have a desk, kettle and hairdryer but no wardrobe.

The Terrace Suites are larger and have a private outdoor terrace, with umbrella, comfortable seats and a decadent open-air shower in a claw-footed bath. There are many up-market restaurants, casual cafes and bars in the area.

**5footway.inn Project Chinatown 1** ** 63 Pagoda Street; http://www.5footwayinn.com/links/project-chinatown-1/

This is one of the favorite hostels and budget accommodations for travelers due to its modern design, coziness, friendly staff, and location in Chinatown just next to the MRT station. There are bunk beds in dorms with individual reading lights and some twin rooms. Guests have access to a shared toilet and bathroom with free toiletries and hot/cold shower and there is a female-only bathroom.

The hostel has an outdoor terrace and a cozy lounge, TV, and free use of a computer. Free hot beverages are available all day and there is a basic free daily breakfast. Self-service laundry services are available at an extra charge. The 24-hour reception offers luggage storage services.

**Tree In Lodge** ** 2 Tan Quee Lan St.; http://www.treeinlodge.com/

This is an environmentally-conscious hostel, with a thoughtful layout and central location 200 meters from Bugis MRT Station (EW12/DT14). Curtains on every bed guarantee privacy whether you're in six- or 12-bedded mixed dorms and the female-only room has its own bathroom. There is a lounge with Wi-Fi, and a range of games and books are available.

**Drop Inn** ** 253 Lavender St.; http://dropinnsingapore.com/

With comfy dorms and plenty of communal space, the Drop Inn is good for backpackers and budget travelers. Accommodation is available in both private and dormitory air-conditioned rooms. The private rooms are spacious but share the same bathrooms as the dorms.

Rates include a Continental breakfast, Wi-Fi, and use of the common room with a book exchange, computers, and movies. A microwave is available in the share kitchen. The hostel is 200 meters from the Lavender Food Market and Boon Keng MRT Station (NE9).

*************************************************

If you have enjoyed this book, please give us a brief review on the Amazon web site so that others will be encouraged to also enjoy it. Just go to www.amazon.com, type in Len Rutledge in the search box. All the Experience Guides will come up, select Experience Singapore 2016, and type a brief review.

This was the seventh book in the **Experience** series. There are a further seven books available as e-books or paperbacks.

We hope you also enjoy the other books in the series:

Experience Thailand e-book; http://www.amazon.com/Experience-Thailand-2016-Guides-ebook/dp/B01911VVBU/

Experience Norway e-book; http://www.amazon.com/Experience-Norway-2016-Guides-ebook/dp/B01A2PHMQM/

Experience Norway paperback; http://www.amazon.com/Experience-Norway-2016-Guides/dp/151958959X/

Experience Northern Italy e-book; http://www.amazon.com/Experience-Northern-Italy-2016-Guides-ebook/dp/B01BA6E526/

Experience Northern Italy paperback; http://www.amazon.com/Experience-Northern-Italy-2016-Guides/dp/1523809949/

Experience Ireland e-book; http://www.amazon.com/Experience-Ireland-2016-Guides-Book-ebook/dp/B01BESWSJ2/

Experience Myanmar (Burma) e-book; http://www.amazon.com/Experience-Myanmar-Burma-2016-Guides-ebook/dp/B01A2X781S/

Experience Myanmar (Burma) paperback; http://www.amazon.com/Experience-Myanmar-Burma-2016-Guides/dp/1522829652/

Experience Istanbul e-book; http://www.amazon.com/Experience-Istanbul-2016-Guides-ebook/dp/B01CNJ6MTS/

Experience Singapore e-book; http://www.amazon.com/Experience-Singapore-2016-Guides-Book-ebook/dp/B01BXUWCME/

Experience India's Golden Triangle; http://www.amazon.com/dp/B00T9KR1I6

We welcome comments from readers. Please send them by email to len_rutledge@bigpond.com

# Index

# ABOUT THE AUTHOR

Len Rutledge has been travel writing for 40 years. During that time he has written thousands of newspaper articles, numerous magazine pieces, more than a thousand web reviews and around 30 travel guide books. He has worked with Pelican Publishing, Viking Penguin, Berlitz, the Rough Guide and the Nile Guide amongst others.

Along the way he has started a newspaper, a travel magazine, a Visitor and TV guide and completed a PhD in tourism. His travels have taken him to more than 100 countries and his writings have collected a PATA award, an ASEAN award, an IgoUgo Hall of Fame award and other recognition.

You can see more details on the author's website: www.LenRutledge.com

# ABOUT THE PHOTOGRAPHER

Phensri Rutledge was born in Thailand but has lived in Australia for many years. For 30 years her photographs have appeared in a range of guidebooks and in newspapers and magazines in Europe, North America, Asia and Australia. Her travels have taken her to all continents except Antarctica through over 80 countries.

She contributes to several travel web sites and has a number of popular social media sites including a Google+ site with over 2.5 million views and thousands of followers. See http://google.com/+PhensriRutledge

Made in the USA
Lexington, KY
02 August 2016